Journal of Early Childhood and Infant Psychology

Volume 7
2011

PACE UNIVERSITY PRESS   NEW YORK

ISSN 1554-6144
ISBN 978-1-935625-09-4

Address Subscription Inquiries to:

Pace University Press
41 Park Row, Room 1510
New York, NY 10038

www.pace.edu/press
(212) 346-1405

Journal of Early Childhood and Infant Psychology

Editorial Policy: The Journal of Early Childhood and Infant Psychology (JECIP) is a publication of the Association of Early Childhood and Infant Psychologists (AECIP). One aspect of AECIP's mission is to provide a vehicle for networking within early childhood and infant psychology, including fostering research, scholarship, and professional interactions. This journal (JECIP) focuses on publishing original contributions from a broad range of psychological perspectives relevant to infants, young children (up to age 8), parents, and caregivers. Manuscripts incorporating evidence-based research, theory and applications within clinical, community, developmental, neurological, and school psychology perspectives are considered. In addition to data-based research, the journal accepts test and book reviews, position statements, literature reviews, program descriptions and evaluations, clinical studies, and other professional materials of interest to psychologists working with infants, young children, parents, families, and caregivers. Proposals for mini-series may be made to the Editor.

Format: Manuscripts should be original work not currently submitted for publication to other journals. Authors must follow the guidelines of the *Publication Manual of the American Psychological Association (Sixth Edition)*. Manuscripts may not exceed 35 double-spaced pages in length, including the cover page, abstract, references, tables and figures.

Submission: Submit an electronic copy of the manuscript for editorial review. Avoid including any identifying author information in the text. Selection of manuscripts is based on blind peer review. Include a cover page with the following information: the title of article, author(s) full name(s), title(s), institution or professional affiliations, and mailing and email address of primary author. The cover page will not be sent to reviewers.

Selection Criteria:
- Importance of topic in early childhood and infant psychology
- Theory and research related to content
- Contribution to professional practice in early childhood and infant psychology
- Clear and concise writing

Submit manuscripts to the Editor at the following address:
Anastasia E. Yasik
Editor, JECIP
Psychology Department, Pace University
41 Park Row
New York, New York 10038
(212) 346-1801
Email: jecip@pace.edu

Journal of
Early
Childhood and
Infant
Psychology

Volume 7, 2011

Kate Driscoll & Robert C. Pianta	1	Mothers' and Fathers' Perceptions of Conflict and Closeness in Parent-Child Relationships during Early Childhood
Jillian L. Childres, Heather Agazzi, & Kathleen Armstrong	25	Evaluating Outcomes of a Behavioral Parent Training Program for Caregivers of Young Children: Waitlist-Control vs. Immediate Treatment
Rachel Bowman & Joseph R. Scotti	45	Development of the Quality of Life Questionnaire for Families of Young Children with Developmental Delays
Lia E. Sandilos & James C. DiPerna	65	Interrater Reliability of the Classroom Assessment Scoring System – Pre-K (CLASS Pre-K)

Masha Y. Ivanova, Thomas
M. Achenbach, Leslie A.
Rescorla, Niels Bilenberg,
Gudrun Bjarnadottir, Silvia
Denner, Pedro Dias, Anca
Dobrean, Manfred Doepfner,
Elaheh Mohammad Esmaeili,
Alessandra Frigerio, Halldor
S. Gudmundsson, Roma
Jusiene, Solvejg Kristensen,
Felipe Lecannelier, Patrick W.
L. Leung, VÂnia Sousa Lima,
Jianghong Liu, Sofia P. Lobel,
Barbara Cesar Machado,
Jasminka Markovic, Paola A.
Mas, Rosario Montirosso, Julia
Plueck, Adelina A. Pronaj,
Jorge T. Rodrigquez, Pamela O.
Rojas, Klaus Schmeck, Mimoza
Shahini, Jaime R. Silva,
Jan van der Ende, & Frank C.
Verhulst

87

Syndromes of Preschool
Psychopathology Reported by
Teachers and Caregivers in 14
Societies Using the Caregiver-
Teacher Report Form (C-TRF)

Sarah E. Martin, Mari L.
Clements, & Keith A. Crnic

105

Internalizing and Externalizing
Symptoms in Two-Year-Olds:
Links to Mother-Toddler
Emotion Processes

Mothers' and Fathers' Perceptions of Conflict and Closeness in Parent-Child Relationships during Early Childhood

Kate Driscoll, Ph.D., & Robert C. Pianta, Ph.D.
University of Virginia

The Child-Parent Relationship Scale (CPRS) was used to describe the stability and consistency of parents' perceptions of their relationships with their children ($N = 563$) across 3 years during the preschool to elementary school period for children enrolled in the NICHD Study of Early Child Care and Youth Development. Research questions pertained to stability of ratings and differences in reports for gender of parent and child. Another goal of the study was to further examine the psychometric properties of the CPRS, a 15-item self-report instrument assessing relational conflict and closeness. Maternal and paternal ratings of closeness and conflict were somewhat stable across this period. Mothers reported higher levels of closeness and conflict with both boys and girls at both 54 months and first grade than did fathers. Consistency between mothers' and fathers' reports was moderate and was higher for conflict than for closeness. Levels of parent agreement were dependent upon the gender of the child. Fathers reported more closeness with daughters than with sons, and they experienced an increase in their feelings of closeness with their children during this period, relative to mothers. Results are discussed in light of research on parent-child relationships and parents' perceptions. It is important to note that findings from this study reflect data collected from families with both a mother and father present during this 3-year period.

The quality of the relational bond between parent and child affects children's emotional development, school performance, and social growth. Parents perceive their relationships with their children in a variety of ways and numerous researchers have attempted to assess these connections. This study investigated the stability of mothers' and fathers' perceptions of parent-child relationships with sons and daughters across 3 years during the transition to school. This study describes stability and patterns of parents' perceptions across time, gender, and informant in terms of dimensions of relational conflict and closeness. The results have implications for understanding how parents have different relational experiences with sons and daughters.

Correspondence concerning this article should be addressed to: Kate Driscoll, Ph.D., Children's Hospital Boston, 300 Longwood Avenue, Boston, MA 02115. E-mail: katherine.driscoll@childrens.harvard.edu

Parent-Child Relationships and Child Development

The following section reviews current literature on parent-child relationships as they relate to children's emotional, academic, and social outcomes. The relationship between a child and his or her parents forms a foundation for all other interpersonal relationships. Bowlby (1982) suggested that parents' behavior in parent-child relationships is guided by an underlying system, referred to as the caregiving system, and remarked, "the study of caregiving as a behavioral system, differing somewhat between mothers and fathers, is an enterprise calling for attention" (p. 376). The caregiving behavioral system between parent and child is in part composed of parents' internal representations of relationships of the child and of caregiving. Bowlby's concepts have been developed in recent years by numerous attachment researchers (e.g., Bretherton, Biringen, Ridgeway, Maslin, & Sherman, 1989; George & Solomon, 1991, 1996; Slade & Cohen, 1996; Solomon & George 1996; Solomon, George & De Jong, 1995; Zeanah, Benoit, Hirshberg, Barton, & Regan, 1995) who view the development of parents' representations in relating with the child as intrinsic to the development of the caregiving relationship and key features of their caregiving behavior. Relational representations can affect children's emotional development, school performance, and social growth.

Numerous studies demonstrate the important role that the parent-child relationship plays in predicting academic performance during the early school years (e.g., Barth & Parke, 1993; de Ruiter & van IJzendoorn, 1993; Greenberg & Speltz, 1988; Pianta, 1997, 1999). For example, preschool age measures of mother-child interaction have been shown to be more predictive of special education referrals in school than were standardized tests (Pianta, Erickson, Wagner, Kreutzer, & Egeland, 1990; Wagner, 1993). Accurate measures of parent-child relationships could aid in the identification of children who are at-risk for school adjustment problems (Pianta & Harbers, 1996). Testing a conceptual model of a psychosocial pathway to academic competence in preschool, Wood (2007) found that early secure attachments to parents were associated with decreased anxiety, removing emotional barriers to learning.

Parental sensitivity and stimulation are two specific characteristics of families that are empirically associated with children's abilities upon school entry (Comer & Haynes, 1991; Downer & Pianta, 2006; Estrada, Arsenio, Hess, & Holloway, 1985; National Institute of Child Health and Human Development [NICHD] Early Child Care Research Network, 2003; Pianta & Harbers, 1996; Pianta, Smith, & Reeve, 1991; Ramey & Campbell, 1991). Specifically, parents' sensitive caregiving, ample learning materials, opportunities for cognitive stimulation, and predictable routines facilitate children's motivation to learn, self-regulation, language, literacy, and social-emotional development. In another study using this NICHD sample, maternal sensitivity was found to have the strongest associations with social-emotional outcomes (NICHD Early Child Care Research Network). Specifically, mothers' observed sensitivity with children at 54 months and kindergarten was related to increased social competence, fewer problem behaviors, and less conflict with adults. Increases in maternal sensitivity during the infant, toddler, and preschool years were also positively associated with children's emotional functioning in kindergarten.

The development of competent relationships with peers is viewed as one of the most important tasks of childhood (Asher & Gottman, 1981; Black & Logan, 1995; Kupersmidt, Coie, & Dodge, 1990; Ladd, 1989), and children's daily interactions with their parents, including shared pretend play, humor, negotiation of conflict, enforcement of behavioral standards, and family conversations provide children with a natural context in which to learn about the social world (Hastings & Rubin, 1999; Laible & Thompson, 2000; Thompson, 1998). Attachment theorists have also stressed the importance of parent-child connections in a child's education about self and others (Laible & Thompson, 2000). Wood (2007) found that early secure attachment to parents enhanced positive peer relationships and academic competence. Mothers' perceptions of their children as more or less trusting and secure predict children's peer acceptance in preschool (Wood, Emerson, & Cowan, 2004). Parenting systems of involvement, warmth, and directiveness have been associated with variations in children's social competence (Booth, Rose-Krasnor, McKinnon, & Rubin, 1994; Hastings & Rubin, 1999; McFadyen-Ketchum, Bates, Dodge, & Petit, 1996), while parent-child relationships characterized by hostility have been associated with negative social outcomes. The children of parents who are rejecting, angry, or uninvolved are more likely to be socially rejected by their peers than children of warm, involved parents who consistently enforce rules (Cohn, 1990; McDonald & Parke, 1984; Putallaz, 1987). Insecurely attached boys tend to be less well liked by classmates and teachers and were perceived as more aggressive by their peers (Cohn).

Parent-child relationships frequently serve as assets, moderators, and mediators (Sroufe, Duggal, Weinfield, & Carlson, 2000) when children are faced with specific risks. Protective factors moderate the impact of risk variables (Rutter, 1990), while assets or "promotive" factors are variables that are regularly associated with positive outcomes (Sameroff, 1997). The same factor may be regarded as an asset or protective factor, depending on the context (Sroufe et al.). The most extensively researched assets and protective factors in the parent-child relationship are parental warmth and emotional support, and the security of the attachment between infant and caregiver. Numerous studies have demonstrated the connection between parental warmth and healthy emotional development during childhood (e.g., Campbell, 1997; Hetherington & Clingempeel, 1992; Sroufe, 1997). Attachment security has been linked with later self-esteem, social competence, prosocial behavior, ego resiliency, and overall adjustment (Sroufe, 1997).

Assessment of Parent-Child Relationships

Parents' representations, or perceptions, of their relationships with their children have been assessed by interviews, coding systems, observations, and questionnaires. Several significant issues arise in the evaluation of parent-child relationships. Before outlining the major issues within the field of early parent-child relationships, it is important to define what is meant by *relationship*. Relationships have been described as a particular form of a system (Hinde, 1987; Pianta, 1997; Sameroff & Emde, 1989). A parent-child relationship is not equal to the sum of the exchanges between them, or their traits as individuals (Pianta, 1997); they possess their own identity aside from the attributes of interactions or individuals (Sroufe, 1989). Of relationships, Pianta (1997) writes: "Relationships have a history, a memory; they are patterns of interactions, expectations, beliefs and affects organized at a level more abstract than observable behaviors" (p. 14). He stresses the importance of assessing relationships over time and across situations in order to more fully describe and understand these qualities (Pianta, 1997).

The major issues to explore within this topic are relationship assessment; stability across time, gender, conflict and closeness in early childhood relationships; and consistency across reporters. Each of these issues affects the assessment of early parent-child relationships and it is necessary to explore these matters and how they influence evaluation. These topics undoubtedly shape current research and theory in the area of early parent-child relationships. Recent findings on each subject will be explored in the following section.

Relationship Assessment

In recent years, several research groups have introduced both interviews and coding systems that are designed to assess and rate parental representations of the child (Aber, Slade, Berger, Bresgi, & Kaplan, 1985; George & Solomon, 1989, 1996; Zeanah, Benoit, Hirshberg, Barton, & Regan, 1995). Interviews often ask parents to describe their relationship with their child in detail, and then focus on parents' responses to emotionally charged interactions, their understanding of the child's experience, and their ability to reflect on the nature of their response to their child (Slade, Belsky, Aber, & Phelps, 1999). In the majority of developmental and clinical research, mother-child interaction has been assessed using carefully controlled laboratory assessments, extended analysis of behavior in naturalistic environments, or coding of discrete behaviors (Barth & Parke, 1993; Mash & Terdal, 1988; Pianta & Harbers, 1996).

Research groups have employed different theoretical models when devising their assessment tools. George and Solomon (1989, 1996) put forward two features of the mother's caregiving system that may be reflected in representations. The first is content, and focuses on the mother's view of herself as a caregiver both in general and for a specific child, and how she recognizes the child as necessitating and receiving her care. The other aspect of the caregiving system is the manner in which the mother processes represented information. Both the content of the information and how it is processed can be used as dimensions for organizing representational constructs (Button, Pianta, & Marvin, 2001).

Slade, Belsky, Aber, and Phelps (1999) identified three dimensions of maternal experience in parenting young children. The first dimension pertains to the manner in which mothers represent joy and pleasure in their relationships with their children, and the second relates to how mothers represent anger. The third dimension concerns the way mothers represent guilt and separation distress in their relationships with their children. This approach allows examination of stability and change in the structure, mean levels, and correlates of these dimensions over time (Connell & Furman, 1984). Structural change occurs when the meaning of a specific behavior changes with development, and can be assessed by examining the number and composition of factors. Changes in centrality suggest that times of transition may produce some variables that become less related to each other, while others become more related to each other.

Relationship Stability across Time

When considering the parent-child relationship during childhood, it is essential to contemplate the stability of this connection over time. At the present time, few empirical studies that might provide insight to this question have been conducted. Research in this area has focused primarily on the general concepts of stability and change in relationships and measurements of parental anger and stress across childhood.

Some researchers suggest that relationships and parental attitudes are characterized by change (Goodnow, 1988; Holden & Edwards, 1989), given that attitudes are learned responses that are shaped through interactions with the environment (Holden & Edwards). Attachment theorists suggest that in addition to prior relationship history, daily interactions form a basis for mental representations of others (Main, Kaplan, & Cassidy, 1985; Slade & Aber, 1992). Early childhood is characterized by dramatic changes in children's functioning (Aber & Baker, 1990; Aber, Belsky, Slade, & Crnic, 1999; Lieberman, 1994; Mahler, Pine, & Bergman, 1975; Shimm & Ballen, 1995) which could potentially impact parents' representations of their relationships with their sons and daughters. Furthermore, changes in levels of parenting stress and quality have been associated with changes in children's attachment classifications (Lieberman & Pawl, 1990; Waters, 1978).

Although the focus was on toddlers and not preschoolers, a study of stability and change in maternal representations of mother-toddler relationships concluded that there are significant increases in mothers' levels of anger from 15 to 28 months, and that while relatively stable, relationships during this period are still open to change (Aber et al., 1999). One study of maternal conceptions of rules for toddlers determined that children's levels of compliance increase significantly with age and are greater for property, safety, and interpersonal behaviors (Smetana, Kochanska, & Chuang, 2000). Another study of parents' perceptions of daily parenting hassles indicated that reported hassles are significantly greater with increasing child age (Crnic & Booth, 1991). These contradictory findings suggest that it is unclear whether child compliance or parental hassles increase or decrease with child age. The present study addressed this inconsistency by investigating the stability of conflict and closeness in the parent-child relationship throughout early childhood.

In a recent study, Barry and Kochanska (2010) examined the affective environment in families longitudinally at various points between 7 and 67 months. Parents' emotional expressiveness was highest early in children's development and decreased over time. Children's anger was found to be highest at 15 months and decreased over time. Children's positive emotions, particularly with mothers, increased over time.

Gender

Patterns of relational functioning associated with gender can refer to both the gender of the parent and the gender of the child within the parent-child relationship. It is important to consider gender when investigating early childhood relationships because male and female parents may employ different patterns in their interactions with male and female children. The majority of studies examining parent-child relationships have focused on mother-child relationships rather than father-child relationships. Although empirical studies have not been conducted to determine whether mothers or fathers tend to feel more closeness or conflict with their daughters or sons, several studies do offer ideas about behavioral patterns that do and do not emerge for mothers and fathers of preschoolers.

Mothers and children tend to spend more time together than do fathers and children (Parke, 1995; Russell & Russell, 1987). However, when both parents and child are together, mothers and fathers instigate interaction with children with equal frequency (Noller, 1980; Russell & Russell). Fathers are relatively more involved in physical play interactions while mothers report more caregiving interactions; however, mothers and fathers engage in caregiving to a similar degree in observational studies when both parents are present (Collins, Harris, & Susman, 1995). Mothers' and fathers' parenting styles have been found to be moderately correlated within families (Barnett, Deng, Mills-Koonce, Willoughby, & Cox, 2008; Feinberg, Reiss, Neiderhiser, & Hetherington, 2005).

Both positive and negative emotional expressions and interactions characterized by conflict are more common in mother-child than in father-child interactions (Bronstein, 1984; Russell & Russell, 1987). A possible explanation for this is that mothers spend more time with their children in a greater diversity of shared activities than do fathers (Collins et al., 1995). Although there is some indication that interactions with sons are marked by more affect than those with daughters, whether these emotions are more positive or negative is contradictory across studies (Bronstein; Noller, 1980; Russell & Russell; Salt, 1991).

There is some evidence to support the idea that relationships with daughters involve different emotions than relationships with sons. In a study of gender differences in conversations about emotions, both mothers and fathers used a greater number and variety of emotion words with daughters than with sons and parents mentioned sad aspects of events more with girls than with boys (Kuebli & Fivush, 1992). A study of maternal attitudes determined that protective mothers report that they are more likely to use warmth and involvement to comfort withdrawn daughters than sons (Hastings & Rubin, 1999). Both mothers and fathers perceive similar amounts of hassle in their relationships with their children (Crnic & Booth, 1991). Despite calls for studies of the entire family system (Parke & McDowell, 1998), the majority of research on emotion in parent-child interactions has focused on the mother-child dyad. Studies examining emotions expressed in father-child interactions report both similarities and differences across parents (Bridges & Connell, 1991; McElwain et al., 2007). In sum, mothers and fathers appear to experience both qualitative and quantitative differences in their relationships with their sons and daughters.

Conflict and Closeness in Early Childhood Relationships

The present study focuses on the assessment of conflict and closeness in parent-child relationships, so it is important to consider the patterns of positive and negative emotions that have previously been identified in relationships between parents and children. Several studies have concluded that a mutually responsive parent-child relationship that is characterized by high levels of shared positive affect contributes to a child's readiness to incorporate parental messages and values (Kochanska & Thompson, 1997; Laible & Thompson, 2000; Maccoby, 1984). Strong emotions, both positive and negative, occur daily in the course of parenting (Dix, 1991).

Researchers have speculated that conflict may be an important aspect of children's socialization (Dunn & Slomkowski, 1992; Kuczynski, Kochanska, Radke-Yarrow, & Girnius-Brown, 1987). The increase in parent-child conflict across the toddler and preschool years is well-documented by researchers (e.g. Dunn, 1988; Dunn & Munn, 1985, 1987; Kuczynski et al.; Laible & Thompson, 2002). In a review on the literature on conflict, Dix (1991) suggested that parents with young children are engaged in conflict with them an average of 3.5 to 15 times each hour. Another study reported even higher rates of conflict (Klimes-Dougan & Kopp, 1999). It is important to make the distinction between constructive and destructive conflicts (Hartup & Laursen, 1993; Vandell & Bailey, 1992). Constructive conflict involves high levels of negotiation, justification, and resolution and is likely to enhance development. Conversely, destructive conflict is often a marker of dysfunctional relationships (Laible & Thompson, 2002).

Closeness is also an important predictive factor in the parent-child relationship. Mothers who engage with their children in a warm and responsive manner have children who are described as socially competent, securely attached, and successful in school (Field, 1987; Fiese, Wilder, Bickham, 2000; Grolinck & Ryan, 1989; Sroufe, 1983). Similar patterns of relation have been identified in relation to father-child interactions (Parke, 1981). The positive relationship between parental warmth and child adjustment extends from the toddler years (Belsky, Woodworth, & Crnic, 1996), to the preschool period (Campbell, 1994), to adolescence (Allen, Hauser, O'Connor, Bell, & Eickholt, 1996).

Consistency Across Reporters

When assessing early parent-child relationships, it is important to consider who is reporting the information that is to be assessed, whether that is a mother or a father. At present, few empirical studies have been conducted to determine the consistency of mother-father reports concerning their relationships with their sons and daughters. The majority of studies in this area focus on parental consistency with adolescents rather than preschoolers. One toddler study reported moderate mother-father agreement in ratings of twins' temperaments (Saudino & Cherny, 2001) at 14, 20, 24, and 36 months. Although several studies have investigated consistency between maternal and paternal reports of *behavior*, few studies have considered the association between mother-father reports of *relationships*. The present study further explores the factors of consistency across reporters for sons and daughters.

Present Study

Parents' perceptions of their relationships with their children can serve as key indicators of the quality of the parent-child relationship, which in turn is a robust predictor of children's emotional development, school performance, and social growth. However, the stability of parents' perceptions of parent-child relationships during early childhood and gender differences in perceptions of conflict and closeness levels among mothers, fathers, daughters, and sons have yet to be analyzed. Using mother and father reports of relationships at 54-months and first grade, the present study analyzes the following questions: Are parent-child relationships between 54-months and first grade characterized by stability or change? Do mothers or fathers report higher degrees of conflict or closeness with their daughters or sons?

Do mothers and fathers differ in their representations? Results of this study may offer new information regarding mothers' and fathers' perceptions of their relationships with their children and may have implications for the assessment of parent-child relationships across the early childhood years.

Method

Sample

The participants in the current study were 563 children and their families who were involved in the NICHD Study of Early Child Care, a comprehensive, observational study of key developmental contexts from birth to sixth grade. Families were recruited during postpartum hospital visits to mothers after the birth of a child in 1991 at ten locations in the United States (Little Rock, AR; Irvine, CA; Lawrence, KS; Boston, MA; Philadelphia, PA; Pittsburgh, PA; Charlottesville, VA; Morganton, NC; Seattle, WA; Madison, WI). Recruitment and selection procedures are described in several publications (see NICHD ECCRN, 2002). The present studied involved 563 of the original 1,364 participants in the NICHD study. Participants were included in the present study if mothers and fathers completed the CPRS at 54 months and first grade. Participants included 294 boys and 269 girls. Children of color represent 7% of the sample. Mothers had an average of 15.1 years of education and fathers had an average of 15.3 years of education. It is important to note that findings from this study reflect data collected from families with both a mother and father present during this 3-year period.

Overview of Data Collection

Mothers and fathers were asked to complete questionnaires in the laboratory at 54 months and first grade. Structured interactions between parents and study children were also videotaped in the laboratory at 54 months and first grade visits.

Measures

Child Parent Relationship Scale (CPRS). The CPRS (Pianta, 1998) is a self-report instrument completed by mothers and fathers that assesses parents' perceptions of their relationships with their sons and daughters. The 15 items are rated on a 5-point Likert scale and the ratings can be summed into groups of items corresponding to conflict and closeness subscales.

The 8-item conflict subscale measures the degree to which a parent feels that his or her relationship with a particular child is characterized by negativity. Cronbach *alphas* for maternal conflict were .84 at 54 months and .84 at first grade, while Cronbach *alphas* for paternal conflict were .80 at 54 months and .78 at first grade. The 7-item closeness scale assesses the extent to which a parent feels that the relationship is characterized by warmth, affection, and open communication. Cronbach *alphas* for maternal closeness were .69 at 54 months and .64 at first grade, while Cronbach *alphas* for paternal closeness were .72 at 54 months and .74 at first grade. The conflict and closeness scales of the CPRS represent two distinct domains of parent-child relationships, as evidenced by a relatively low correlation between the scales ($r = .16$).

The CPRS was adapted from the Student Teacher Relationship Scale (STRS; Pianta, 2001), which is an instrument that assesses teachers' perceptions of their relationships with individual students. Items were derived from attachment theory and the attachment Q-set (Waters & Deane, 1985), as well as a review of the literature on teacher-child interactions. The STRS is easily adapted to enable the parent to report the child's attachment behaviors in the home. A goal of the present study is to further examine the psychometric properties of the CPRS.

Validity of CPRS. Structured interactions between parents and study children were videotaped at 54 months and first grade. Videotapes of 499 index children and their mothers or fathers during structured interactions were coded by trained observers. The response categories ranged from 1 to 7 on each of six scales reflecting parent behaviors. Parent ratings included supportive presence, respect for child's autonomy, stimulation of cognitive development, quality of child assistance, hostility of parent toward child, and parent's confidence.

The videotapes of the parent-child interactions were sent to a central collection site for coding. Coders were blind to family information. Inter-coder reliability was determined by assigning two coders 19-20% of the tapes randomly drawn at each assessment period. Coders were unaware of which videotapes were assigned to double coding, and reliability assessments were conducted throughout the period of coding. Inter-coder reliability was calculated as the intra-class correlation coefficient. Reliability for the composite scores exceeded .83 at every age.

The materials for the structured interaction differed for mothers and fathers at both time points. At 54 months, the mother-child interaction was comprised of two challenging tasks (maze, block-building) requiring maternal assistance and one pretend play activity (puppets). The father-child interaction consisted of one challenging task (ramp and marble construction project) and one pretend play activity (jungle animals). At first grade, both parent-child interactions were comprised of three activities incorporating teaching and play (Etch-A-Sketch drawing, pattern block activity, card game).

Correlations among CPRS parental closeness ratings and observer ratings were highest for supportive presence, sensitivity, and positive caregiving. Associations among CPRS parental conflict ratings and observer ratings were highest for hostility. Overall, many statistically significant correlations between parent and observer reports were apparent from analyses; however, the magnitude of the associations were relatively small.

Correlations with Child Behavior Checklist and Social Skills Rating System. Additional validity analyses were conducted to determine correlations with two common validators: the Child Behavior Checklist (CBCL) and the Social Skills Rating System (SSRS). The CBCL is a 118-item measure that addresses a broad range of children's behavioral and emotional problems. Parents completed the measure at both 54 months and first grade. The SSRS includes 38 items that provide a broad multi-rater assessment of social skills and problem behaviors. In the NICHD study, both the social skills and problem behavior portions of the SSRS were administered at 54 months, but the measure was modified at first grade to only include the social skills items. Correlations between CPRS scales and the CBCL and SSRS are reported in Table 1.

CPRS Means and Standard Deviations. CPRS conflict and closeness means and standard deviations for the overall sample ($N = 1070$ mothers at 54 months, 1015 at first grade and 715 fathers at 54 months, 664 at first grade) are reported in this section. Maternal closeness means were 37.28 ($SD = 2.71$) at 54 months and 37.98 ($SD = 2.50$) at first grade. Mothers' ratings of conflict averaged 16.52 ($SD = 5.19$) at 54 months and 15.21 ($SD = 5.87$) at first grade. Paternal closeness means were 35.74 ($SD = 3.19$) at 54 months and 36.93 ($SD = 2.74$) at first grade. Fathers' ratings of conflict averaged 15.46 ($SD = 4.59$) at 54 months and 14.23 ($SD = 4.90$) at first grade.

Table 1

Parental Correlations for CPRS Closeness and Conflict Ratings at 54 Months and First Grade with CBCL and SSRS ratings ($N = 563$)

	54 months		1st grade	
	Close	Conflict	Close	Conflict
Mothers				
SSRS Competence	.348**	-.450**		
SSRS Prob Behavior	-.180**	.509**		
CBCL Externalizing	-.181**	.583**	-.263**	.686**
CBCL Total Probs	-.230**	.526**	-.292**	.615**
Fathers				
SSRS Competence	.410**	-.449**		
SSRS Prob Behavior	-.197**	.436**		
CBCL Externalizing	-.153**	.515**	-.194**	.594**
CBCL Total Probs	-.199**	.479**	-.250**	.549**

$**p < .01$

Data Analysis

The first step in the analysis was to run a series of basic correlations between the CPRS conflict and closeness scores at 54 months and first grade, for mothers and then for fathers. These correlations assessed stability within informants by examining associations of parents' scores across 3 years. Consistency across informants was also assessed by correlating mother's and father's perceptions of their relationships with the study at each occasion. Repeated measures ANOVAs were conducted across time, within informants, and between genders to examine changes or differences in mean levels of conflict and closeness.

Results

Descriptive Results by Informant, Time, and Gender

The following section outlines the associations between maternal and paternal closeness and conflict ratings at 54 months and first grade. Cross-time and within-time statistics are presented. In the first step of the analysis, a series of correlations examined cross-time associations between mothers' ratings of closeness to their children at 54 months and first grade, for boys and then for girls. In addition, correlations examined stability/cross-time associations between fathers' ratings of closeness to their children at 54 months and first grade, for boys and then for girls. For mothers, the correlation between closeness at 54 months and closeness at first grade is .44. For boys, the correlation between closeness at 54 months and closeness at first grade is .37. The correlation between closeness at 54 months and closeness for girls at first grade is .50. For fathers, the correlation between closeness at 54 months and closeness at first grade is .52. The correlation between closeness at 54 months and closeness for boys at first grade is .56. The correlation between closeness at 54 months and closeness for girls at first grade is .46. Results indicate that maternal and paternal ratings of closeness with sons and daughters are moderately stable between 54 months and first grade. All reported correlations are statistically significant at the .01 level.

Next, a series of correlations examined within-time associations between both parents' ratings of closeness to their children at 54 months and first grade, for boys and then for girls. The correlation between mothers' and fathers' ratings of closeness with children at 54 months is .14. The correlation between mothers' and fathers' ratings of closeness with children at first grade is .15. The correlation between mothers' and fathers' ratings of closeness for boys at 54 months is .20. The correlation between mothers' and fathers' ratings of closeness for girls at first grade is .23. All reported correlations are statistically significant at the .01 level. Although there is significant consistency in maternal and paternal closeness ratings for sons and daughters at 54 months and first grade, the magnitude of the association is quite small. Thus, mothers' and fathers' ratings of closeness with the same child do not appear to be strongly related. It is the case, however, that mothers' and fathers' ratings of closeness appear to be more strongly related for sons at 54 months and for daughters at first grade relative to daughters at 54 months and sons at first grade.

The next set of analyses examined associations between mothers' ratings of conflict with their children at 54 months and first grade, for boys and then for girls. In addition, cross-time correlations were run to examine stability of fathers' ratings of conflict with their children at 54 months and first grade, for boys and then for girls. For mothers, the correlation between conflict at 54 months and conflict at first grade is .65. The correlation between conflict at 54 months and conflict for boys at first grade is .67. The correlation between conflict at 54 months and conflict for girls at first grade is .64. For fathers, the correlation between conflict at 54 months and conflict at first grade is .60. The correlation between conflict at 54 months and conflict for boys at first grade is .59. The correlation between conflict at 54 months and conflict for girls at first grade is .61. All reported correlations are statistically significant at the .01 level.

Mothers' ratings of conflict with their sons and daughters are highly stable between 54 months and first grade and are more stable than maternal closeness ratings between 54 months and first grade. Maternal closeness correlations range from .37 to .50, while maternal conflict ratings range from .64 to .67. Results for fathers indicate that paternal ratings of conflict with sons and daughters are moderately to highly stable between 54 months and first grade, and are more stable than paternal closeness ratings between 54 months and first grade. Paternal closeness correlations range from .46 to .56, while paternal conflict ratings range from .59 to .61.

Associations between mothers' and fathers' ratings of conflict with their child at 54 months and first grade, for boys and then for girls, are reported as follows. The correlation between mothers' and fathers' ratings of conflict with children at 54 months is .31. The correlation between mothers' and fathers' ratings of conflict with children at first grade is .30. The correlation between mothers' and fathers' ratings of conflict for boys at 54 months is .28. The correlation between mothers' and fathers' ratings of conflict for girls at 54 months is .36. The correlation between mothers' and fathers' ratings of conflict for boys at first grade is .34. The correlation between mothers' and fathers' ratings of conflict for girls at first grade is .26. All reported correlations are statistically significant at the .01 level.

Results indicate that there is moderate consistency between parents in their perception of conflict with their child. Mothers and fathers show higher levels of agreement among conflict ratings than among closeness ratings. Correlations between maternal and paternal closeness ratings ranged from .14 to .15, while correlations between maternal and paternal conflict ratings ranged from .30 to .31.

Repeated Measures Analyses of Variance (ANOVAs) were conducted to examine change in mean level of closeness and conflict for boys and for girls between

Table 2

Descriptive Statistics for Closeness and Conflict Ratings at 54 Months and First Grade (N = 563, 294 boys and 269 girls)

	54 months		1st grade	
	M	*SD*	*M*	*SD*
Mothers				
Closeness boys	37.59	2.42	38.16	2.06
Closeness girls	37.44	2.49	38.22	2.27
Conflict boys	15.95	5.00	14.80	5.71
Conflict girls	16.36	5.18	15.12	6.09
Fathers				
Closeness boys	35.57	3.25	36.70	2.88
Closeness girls	36.09	2.90	37.21	2.58
Conflict boys	15.67	4.51	14.34	4.83
Conflict girls	15.06	4.40	14.02	4.88

Note: Possible scores range from 8 to 40

54 months and first grade. Time and reporter were within-subjects factors, while gender was a between-subjects factor. Means for maternal and paternal ratings for sons and daughters at 54 months and first grade are presented in Table 2. Results of these analyses for closeness indicate that there were main effects for time, $F(1, 562) = 116.11, p < .01$, and reporter, $F(1, 562) = 137.63, p < .01$. Mothers and fathers reported higher levels of closeness with their children at first grade than at 54 months. Mothers reported more closeness than fathers did at both times and with both sons and daughters. There were significant interactions between reporter and gender, $F(1, 562) = 5.13, p < .05$, and between time and reporter, $F(1, 562) = 8.74, p < .01$. Although mothers reported more closeness than fathers with both sons and daughters, fathers reported more closeness with daughters than with sons. Relative to mothers, fathers demonstrated a significant increase in their closeness ratings between 54 months and first grade for both boys and girls.

Results of analyses for conflict indicate that there were main effects for time, $F(1, 562) = 74.64, p < .01$, and reporter, $F(1, 562) = 12.61, p < .01$. Mothers and fathers reported less conflict with their children at first grade than at 54 months. Mothers reported more conflict than fathers did at both times and with both sons and daughters.

Discussion

The purpose of this study was to examine parents' self-reported perceptions of their relationships with their children during the preschool to elementary school period. Individual differences in mothers' and fathers' ratings of closeness and conflict with their children are somewhat stable during this period, while levels of closeness increase and levels of conflict decrease. Parents' perceptions of their overall relationships with their children appear to become more positive over time during this period. Consistency between maternal and paternal reports is moderate, and is higher for conflict than for closeness. Overall, parents demonstrate more agreement regarding ratings of conflict than ratings of closeness. There are significant differences in the way that mothers and fathers experience closeness in their relationships with their sons and daughters. It is important to note that findings from this study reflect data collected from families with both a mother and father present during this 3-year period.

Parent-Child Relationship Stability across Early Childhood

Results indicate that maternal and paternal ratings of closeness and conflict with sons and daughters are fairly stable between 54 months and first grade, and ratings of conflict are more stable than ratings of closeness for both mothers and fathers. Mean levels of conflict and closeness showed that mothers and fathers reported higher levels of closeness and lower ratings of conflict between 54 months and first grade for both boys and girls. These results are consistent with the results of Smetana, Kochanska, and Chuang (2000) who concluded that children's levels of compliance increase significantly with age in a study of maternal conceptions of rules for toddlers. Results are also consistent with those of Pianta and Stuhlman (2004) concerning teacher-child relationships during this period.

Consistency between Maternal and Paternal Reports

Mothers' and fathers' consistency in their ratings of closeness and conflict at 54 months and first grade was significant, although associations were small, even for ratings of the same child. The association between maternal and paternal reports of closeness was stronger for sons at 54 months and for daughters at first grade. Mothers and fathers showed higher levels of agreement for ratings of conflict than ratings of closeness, suggesting that parents demonstrate greater concurrence regarding issues pertaining to conflict than matters of closeness. These results are consistent with those of Crnic and Booth (1991), who concluded that mothers and fathers perceive similar amounts of hassle in their relationships with their children. Results are also consistent with Parke (1995) and Russell and Russell (1987), who concluded that mothers spend more time with their children than do fathers.

Mothers reported higher levels of closeness and conflict for both boys and girls at both 54 months and first grade. These results are consistent with those of Bronstein (1984) and Russell and Russell (1987), who reported that both positive and negative emotional expressions and interactions characterized by conflict occur more frequently in mother-child than in father-child interactions. A possible justification for this is that mothers spend more time with their children in a greater diversity of activities than do fathers (Collins et al., 1995).

Although mothers reported more closeness than fathers with both boys and girls, some significant patterns of differences emerged for paternal ratings. Fathers reported more closeness with girls than with boys at both time periods. This finding suggests that fathers experience more closeness in their relationships with their daughters than with their sons. In addition, relative to mothers, fathers' ratings of closeness showed a greater increase between 54 months and first grade. Although mothers demonstrated an increase in perceptions of closeness, this finding suggests that the transition to school is characterized by an increase in father-child closeness. These results are consistent with previous findings (Hastings & Rubin,1999; Kuebli & Fivush, 1992) that suggest that mothers and fathers experience differences in their relationships with sons and daughters.

Overall, parents demonstrate greater agreement regarding ratings of conflict than ratings of closeness. On the subject of conflict, parents tend to view the same child in a similar fashion over time, whether that child is male or female. Parents show more signs of disagreement regarding closeness. Levels of parent agreement are dependent on the gender of the child. According to results of this study, fathers experience more closeness with their daughters than with their sons during the preschool to elementary school period. They also experience an increase in their feelings of closeness with their children during this time period, relative to mothers.

Conclusion

Results of this investigation indicate that maternal and paternal ratings of conflict and closeness are somewhat stable during the preschool to elementary school period. Consistency between mothers' and fathers' reports is moderate, and is higher for conflict than for closeness. Mothers report higher levels of closeness and conflict with both sons and daughters at both 54 months and first grade. Mothers and fathers demonstrate more agreement regarding ratings of conflict than ratings of closeness. Levels of parent agreement are dependent upon the gender of the child. Fathers report more closeness with their daughters than with their sons, and, relative to mothers, they experience an increase in their feelings of closeness with their children during this time period. The results of this study have implications for clinical work and research on parent-child relationships. Clinicians working with parents and young children can apply results as they address transition issues with families. A number of research projects are currently using the CPRS to collect data related to parent-child relationships. The study provides a unique contribution to the literature on parent-child relationships, as fathers' relationships with their children tend to be understudied. In addition, preliminary psychometric data obtained regarding the CPRS support further research with the instrument. It is important to note that findings from this study reflect data collected from families with both a mother and father present during this 3-year period. Additional studies using the instrument with a variety of family compositions will provide valuable information.

References

Aber, J. L., & Baker, A. (1990). Security of attachment in toddlerhood: Modifying assessment procedures for joint clinical and research purposes. In M. Greenberg, D. Cicchetti, & M. Cummings (Eds.), *Attachment in the preschool years* (pp. 427-460). Chicago: University of Chicago Press.

Aber, J. L., Belsky, J., Slade, A., & Crnic, K. (1999). Stability and change in mothers' representations of their relationship with their toddlers. *Developmental Psychology, 35,* 1038-1047.

Aber, J. L., Slade, A., Berger, B., Bresgi, I., & Kaplan, M. (1985). *The Parent Development Interview.* Unpublished manuscript.

Allen, J. P., Hauser, S. T., O'Connor, T. G., Bell, K. L., & Eickholt, C. (1996). The connection of observed hostile family conflict to adolescents' developing autonomy and relatedness with parents. *Development and Psychopathology, 8,* 425-442.

Asher, S. R., & Gottman, J. M. (1981). *The development of children's friendships.* New York: Cambridge University Press.

Barnett, M. A., Deng, M., Mills-Koonce, W. R., Willoughby, M., & Cox, M. (2008). Interdependence of parenting of mothers and fathers of infants. *Journal of Family Psychology, 22,* 561-573.

Barry, R. A., & Kochanska, G. (2010). A longitudinal investigation of the affective environment in families with young children: From infancy to early school age. *Emotion, 10,* 237-249.

Barth, J. M., & Parke, R. D. (1993). Parent-child relationship influences on children's transition to school. *Merrill-Palmer Quarterly, 39,* 173-195.

Belsky, J., Woodworth, S., & Crnic, K. (1996). Trouble in the second year: Three questions about family interaction. *Child Development, 67,* 556-578.

Black, B. & Logan, A. (1995). Links between communication patterns in mother-child, father-child, and child-peer interactions and children's social status. *Child Development, 66,* 255-271.

Booth, C. L., Rose-Krasnor, L., McKinnon, J., & Rubin, K. H. (1994). Predicting social adjustment in middle childhood: The role of preschool attachment security and maternal style. *Social Development, 3,* 189-204.

Bowlby, J. (1982). *Attachment and loss: Vol. 1. Attachment* (2nd ed.). New York: Basic Books.

Bretherton, I., Biringen, Z., Ridgeway, D., & Maslin, C. (1989). Attachment: The parental perspective. *Infant Mental Health Journal, 10,* 203-221.

Bronstein, P. (1984). Differences in mothers' and fathers' behaviors toward children: A cross-cultural comparison. *Developmental Psychology, 20,* 995-1003.

Button, S., Pianta, R. C., & Marvin, R.S. (2001). Mothers' representations of relationships with their children: Relations with parenting behavior, mother characteristics, and child disability status. *Social Development, 10,* 455-472.

Campbell, S. B. (1994). Hard-to-manage preschool boys: Externalizing behavior, social competence, and family context at two-year follow-up. *Journal of Abnormal Child Psychology, 22,* 147-166.

Campbell, S. B. (1997). Behavior problems in preschool children: Developmental and family issues. *Advances in Clinical Child Psychology, 19,* 1-26.

Cohn, D. A. (1990). Child-mother attachment of six-year-olds and social competence at school. *Child Development, 61,* 152-162.

Collins, W. A., Harris, M. L., & Susman, A. (1995). Parenting during middle childhood. In M. Bornstein (Ed.), *Handbook of parenting* (pp. 65-89). Mahwah, NJ: Lawrence Erlbaum.

Comer, J. P., & Haynes, N. M. (1991). Parent involvement in schools: An ecological approach. *The Elementary School Journal, 91,* 271-277.

Connell, J. P., & Furman, W. (1984). The study of transitions: Conceptual and methodological considerations. In R. Emde & R. Harmon (Eds.), *Continuity and discontinuity in development* (pp. 153-173). New York: Plenum Press.

Crnic, K. A., & Booth, C. L. (1991). Mother and father perceptions of parenting daily hassles across early childhood. *Journal of Marriage and the Family, 53,* 1042-1050.

de Ruiter, C., & van IJzendoorn, M. H. (1993). Attachment and cognition: A review of the literature. *International Journal of Educational Research, 19,* 5-20.

Dix, T. (1991). The affective organization of parenting: Adaptive and maladaptive processes. *Psychological Bulletin, 110,* 3-25.

Downer, J. T., & Pianta, R. C. (2006). Academic and cognitive functioning in first grade: Associations with earlier home and child care predictors and with concurrent home and classroom experiences. *School Psychology Review, 35,* 11-30.

Dunn, J. (1988). *The beginnings of social understanding.* Cambridge, MA: Harvard University Press.

Dunn, J., & Munn, P. (1985). Becoming a family member: Family conflict and the development of social understanding in the second year. *Child Development, 56,* 480-492.

Dunn, J., & Munn, P. (1987). Development of justification in disputes with mother and sibling. *Developmental Psychology, 23,* 791-798.

Dunn, J., & Slomkowski, C. (1992). Conflict and the development of social understanding. In C. Shantz & W. Hartup (Eds.), *Conflict in child and adolescent development* (pp. 70-92). New York: Cambridge University Press.

Estrada, P., Arsenio, W. F., Hess, R. D., & Holloway, S. D. (1985). Affective quality of the mother-child relationship: Longitudinal consequences for children's school-relevant cognitive functioning. *Developmental Psychology, 23,* 210-215.

Feinberg, M. E., Reiss, D., Neiderhiser, J. M., & Hetherington, E. M. (2005). Differential association of family subsystem negativity on siblings' maladjustment: Using behavior genetic methods to test process theory. *Journal of Family Psychology, 19,* 601-610.

Field, T. M. (1987). Affective and interactive disturbances in infants. In J. Osofosky (Ed.), *Handbook of infant development* (2nd ed., pp. 972-1005). New York: Wiley.

Fiese, B. H., Wilder, J., & Bickham, N. L. (2000). Family context in developmental psychopathology. In A. Sameroff, M. Lewis, & S. Miller (Eds.), *Handbook of developmental psychopathology* (pp. 115-134). New York: Plenum.

George, C., & Solomon, J. (1989). Internal working models of parenting and security of attachment at age six. *Infant Mental Health Journal, 17,* 222-237.

George, C., & Solomon, J. (1991, April). *Children's representations of practicing family using a doll play technique.* Paper presented at the biennial meeting of the Society for Research in Child Development, Seattle, WA.

George, C., & Solomon, J. (1996). Representational models of relationships: Links between caregiving and attachment. *Infant Mental Health Journal, 17,* 198-217.

Goodnow, J. (1988). Parents' ideas, actions, and feelings: Models and methods from developmental and social psychology. *Child Development, 59,* 286-320.

Greenberg, M. T., & Speltz, M. L. (1988). Attachment and the ontogeny of conduct problems. In J. Belsky & T. Nezworski (Eds.), *Clinical implications of attachment* (pp. 177-228). Hillsdale, NJ: Erlbaum.

Grolinck, W. S., & Ryan, R. M. (1989). Parent styles associated with children's self-regulation and competence in school. *Journal of Educational Psychology, 81,* 143-154.

Hartup, W., & Laursen, B. (1993). Conflict and context in peer relations. In C. Hart (Ed.), *Children on playgrounds: Research perspectives and applications* (pp. 44-84). Ithaca, NY: SUNY Press.

Hastings, P. D., & Rubin, K. H. (1999). Predicting mothers' beliefs about preschool-aged children's social behavior: Evidence for maternal attitudes moderating child effects. *Child Development, 70,* 722-741.

Hetherington, E. M., & Clingempeel, W. S. (1992). Coping with marital transitions: A family systems perspective. *Monographs of the Society for Research in Child Development, 57* (2-3. Serial No. 227).

Hinde, R. (1987). *Individuals, relationships, and culture.* New York: Cambridge University Press.

Holden, G. W., & Edwards, L. A. (1989). Parental attitudes toward child rearing: Instruments, issues, and implications. *Psychological Bulletin, 106,* 29-58.

Klimes-Dougan, B., & Kopp, C. (1999). Children's conflict tactics with mothers: A longitudinal investigation of the toddler and preschool years. *Merrill-Palmer Quarterly, 45,* 226-242.

Kochanska, G., & Thompson, R. (1997). The emergence and development of conscience in toddlerhood and early childhood. In J. El Grusec & L. Kuczynski (Eds.), *Parenting strategies and children's internalization of values: A handbook of theoretical and research perspectives* (pp. 53-77). New York: Wiley.

Kuczynski, L., Kochanska, G. Radke-Yarrow, M., & Girnius-Brown, O. (1987). A developmental interpretation of young children's noncompliance. *Developmental Psychology, 23,* 799-806.

Kuebli, J., & Fivush, R. (1992). Gender differences in parent-child conversations about past emotions. *Sex Roles, 27,* 683-698.

Kupersmidt, J. B., Coie, J. D., & Dodge, K. A. (1990). Predicting disorder from peer social problems. In S. R. Asher & J. D. Coie (Eds.), *Peer rejection in childhood* (pp. 274-338). New York: Cambridge University Press.

Ladd, G. W. (1989). Toward a further understanding of peer relationships and their contributions to child development. In T. L. Bernt & G. W. Ladd (Eds.), *Peer relationships in child development* (pp. 1-11). New York: Wiley.

Laible, D. J., & Thompson, R. A. (2000). Mother-child discourse, attachment security, shared positive affect, and early conscience development. *Child Development, 71,* 1424-1440.

Laible, D. J., & Thompson, R. A. (2002). Mother-child conflict in the toddler years: Lessons in emotion, morality, and relationships. *Child Development, 73,* 1187-1203.

Lieberman, A. F. (1994). *The emotional life of the toddler.* New York: Free Press.

Lieberman, A. F., & Pawl, J. H. (1990). Disorders of attachment and secure base behavior in the second year of life: Conceptual issues and clinical intervention. In M. T. Greenberg, D. Cicchetti, & E. M. Cummings (Eds.), *Attachment in the preschool years* (pp. 375-398). Chicago: University of Chicago Press.

Maccoby, E. (1984). Socialization and developmental change. *Child Development, 55,* 317-328.

Mahler, M., Pine, F., & Bergman, A. (1975). *The psychological birth of the human infant: Symbiosis and individuation.* New York: Basic Books.

Main, M., Kaplan, N., & Cassidy, J. (1985). Security in infancy, childhood, and adulthood: A move to the level of representation. *Monographs of the society for research in child development, 50,* 66-104.

Mash, E., & Terdal, L. (1988). *Behavioral assessment of childhood disorders.* New York: Guilford.

McDonald, K. B., & Parke, R. D. (1984). Bridging the gap: Parent-child play interaction and interactive competence. *Child Development, 55,* 1265-1277.

McFadyen-Ketchum, S. A., Bates, J. E., Dodge, K. A., & Petit, G. S. (1996). Patterns of change in early childhood aggressive-disruptive behavior: Gender differences in predictions from early coercive and affectionate mother-child interactions. *Child Development, 67,* 2417-2433.

National Institute of Child Health and Human Development Early Child Care
    Research Network. (2003). Social functioning in first grade: Prediction from
    home, child care, and concurrent school experience. *Child Development, 74,*
    1639-1662.

Noller, P. (1980). Cross-gender effects in two-child families. *Developmental Psy-
    chology, 16,* 159-160.

Parke, R. D. (1981). *Fathers.* Cambridge, MA: Cambridge University Press.

Parke, R. D. (1995). Fathers and families. In M. Bornstein (Ed.), *Handbook of
    Parenting* (pp. 27-63). Mahwah, NJ: Lawrence Erlbaum.

Pianta, R. C. (1997). Adult-child relationship processes and early schooling. *Early
    Education and Development, 8,* 11-26.

Pianta, R. C. (1999). *Enhancing relationships between children and teachers.*
    Washington, DC: American Psychological Association.

Pianta, R. C. (2001). *Student-teacher relationship scale.* Lutz, FL: Psychological
    Assessment Resources, Inc.

Pianta, R., Erikson, M. F., Wagner, N., Kreutzer, T., & Egeland, B. (1990). Pres-
    chool predictors of referrals for special services: Child-based measures vs.
    mother-child interaction. *School Psychology Review, 19,* 240-250

Pianta, R. C., & Harbers, K. L. (1996). Observing mother and child behavior in a
    problem-solving situation at school entry: Relations with academic achieve-
    ment. *Journal of School Psychology, 34,* 307-322.

Pianta, R. C., Smith, N., & Reeve, R. (1991). Observing mother and child beha-
    vior in a problem-solving situation at school entry: Relations with classroom
    adjustment. *School Psychology Quarterly, 6,* 1-16.

Putallaz, M. (1987). Maternal behavior and children's sociometric status. *Child
    Development, 58,* 324-340.

Ramey, C. T., & Campbell, F. A. (1991). Poverty, early childhood education, and
    academic competence: The Abecedarian experiment. In A. C. Huston (Ed.),
    Children in Poverty: Child development in public policy (pp. 190-221). New
    York: Cambridge University Press.

Russell, G., & Russell, A. (1987). Mother-child and father-child relationships in
    middle childhood. *Child Development, 58,* 1573-1585.

Rutter, M. (1990). Psychosocial resilience and protective mechanisms. In J. Rolf,
    A.S. Masten, D. Cicchetti, K. H. Nuechterlein, & S. Weintraub (Eds.), *Risk
    and protective factors in the development of psychopathology* (pp. 181-214).
    New York: Cambridge University Press.

Salt, R. E. (1991). Affectionate touch between fathers and preadolescent sons.
    Journal of Marriage and the Family, 53, 545-554.

Sameroff, A. (1997, April). *Developmental contributions to the study of psycho-
    pathology.* Master lecture presented at the biennial meetings of the Society
    for Research in Child Development, Washington, DC.

Sameroff, A. J., & Emde, R. (Eds.) (1989). *Relationship disturbances in early childhood: A developmental approach.* New York: Basic Books.

Saudino, K. & Cherny, S. (2001). Sources of continuity and change in observed temperament. In R. N. Emde & J. K. Hewitt (Eds.), *Infancy to early childhood: Genetic and environmental influences on developmental change* (pp. 89-110). New York: Oxford University Press.

Shimm, P. H., & Ballen, K. (1995). *Parenting your toddler.* Reading, MA: Addison-Wesley.

Slade, A., & Aber, J. L. (1992) Attachments, drives and development: Conflicts and convergences in theory. In J. Barron, M. Eagle, & D. Wolitzky, (Eds.), *Interface of Psychoanalysis and Psychology* (pp.154 – 186) APA Publications.

Slade, A., Belsky, J, Aber, J. L., & Phelps, J. L. (1999). Mothers' representations of their relationships with their toddlers: Links to adult attachment and observed mothering. *Developmental Psychology, 35,* 611-619.

Slade, A., & Cohen, L. J. (1996). Processes of parenting and the remembrance of things past. *Infant Mental Health Journal, 17,* 217-238.

Smetana, J. G., Kochanska, G., & Chuang, S. (2000). Mothers' conceptions of everyday rules for young toddlers: A longitudinal investigation. *Merrill-Palmer Quarterly, 46,* 391-416.

Solomon, J., & George, C. (1996). Defining the caregiving system: Toward a theory of caregiving. *Infant Mental Health Journal, 17,* 183-97.

Solomon, J., George, C., & De Jong, A. (1995). Children classified as controlling at age six: Evidence of disorganized representational strategies and aggression at home and at school. *Development and Psychopathology, 7,* 447-464.

Sroufe, L. A. (1983). Infant-caregiver attachment and patterns of adaptation in preschool: The roots of maladaptation and competence. In M. Perlmutter (Ed.), *Minnesota Symposia in Child Psychology, 16* (pp. 41-81). Hillsdale, NJ: Erlbaum.

Sroufe, L. A. (1989). Pathways to adaptation and maladaptation: Psychopathology as developmental deviation. In D. Cicchetti (Ed.), *Emergence of a Discipline: Rochester Symposium on Developmental Psychopathology* (pp. 13-40). Hillsdale, NJ: Erlbaum.

Sroufe, L. A. (1997). Psychopathology as an outcome of development. *Development and Psychopathology, 9,* 251-268.

Sroufe, L. A., Duggal, S., Weinfield, N., & Carlson, E. (2000). Relationships, development, and Psychopathology. In A. Sameroff, M. Lewis, & S. Miller (Eds.), *Handbook of developmental psychopathology* (pp. 75-91). New York: Plenum Publishers.

Thompson, R. (1998). Early sociopersonality development. In N. Eisenberg (Ed.) & W. Damon (Series Ed.), *Handbook of child psychology: Vol. 3. Social, emotional, and personality development* (pp. 25-104). New York: Wiley.

Vandell, D., & Baily, M. (1992). Conflict between siblings. In C. Shantz & W. Hartup (Eds.), *Conflict in child and adolescent development* (pp. 186-215). New York: Cambridge University Press.

Wagner, N. (1993). *Early predictors of referrals for special services in a high-risk sample.* Unpublished doctoral dissertation. Minneapolis, MN: University of Minnesota.

Waters, E. (1978). The reliability and stability of individual differences in infant-mother attachment. *Child Development, 49,* 483-494.

Waters, E., & Deane, K. E. (1985). Defining and assessing individual differences in attachment relationships: Q-methodology and the organization of behavior in infancy and early childhood. In I. Bretherton & E. Waters (Eds.), Growing points of attachment theory and research. *Monographs of the Society for Research in Child Development, 50*(1-2, Serial No. 209), 41-65.

Wood, J. J. (2007). Academic competence in preschool: Exploring the role of close relationships and anxiety. *Early Education and Development, 18,* 223-242.

Wood, J. J., Emmerson, N. A., & Cowan, P. A. (2004). Is early attachment security carried forward into relationships with preschool peers? *British Journal of Developmental Psychology, 22,* 245-253.

Zeanah, C., Benoit, D., Hirshberg, L., Barton, M., & Regan, C. (1995). Mothers' representations of their infants as concordant with infant attachment classifications. *Developmental Issues in Psychiatry and Psychology, 1,* 1-14.

Author Note

This study was part of the NICHD Study of Early Child Care and Youth Development which is directed by a Steering Committee and supported by NICHD through a cooperative agreement (U10). The authors and collaborating investigators wish to extend their appreciation to the families and staff who contributed to this research.

Evaluating Outcomes of a Behavioral Parent Training Program for Caregivers of Young Children: Waitlist Control vs. Immediate Treatment

Jillian L. Childres, Ph.D.
Heather Agazzi, Ph.D.
& Kathleen Armstrong, Ph.D.
University of South Florida

This study evaluated the *Helping Our Toddlers, Developing Our Children's Skills* (HOT DOCS) behavioral parent training program, which is designed to teach caregivers a problem-solving approach to understand and address their children's challenging behavior. Caregivers ($N = 128$) of children between the ages of 17 months and 8 years who displayed challenging behavior were assigned to an immediate treatment group or a waitlist-control group. Caregivers' knowledge, attitudes, stress, and perceptions of their children's behavior were evaluated at pre-test and post-test. Following the intervention, caregivers in the treatment group demonstrated greater gains in knowledge and more significant decreases in the severity of children's behavior than caregivers in the waitlist-control group. No differences in caregivers' perceived stress were found between the groups. These findings suggest that the HOT DOCS parent training program is a promising early intervention for caregivers of young children with early emerging challenging behavior.

Keywords: challenging behavior; early intervention; behavioral parent training; waitlist-control; HOT DOCS

Rates of early emerging challenging behavior in young children (ages 18 months to 7 years) continue to increase each year. Current estimates suggest that nearly 25% of otherwise healthy and typically developing young children have mild to moderate levels of chronic behavior problems (Knapp, Ammen, Arstein-Kerslake, Poulson, & Mastergeorge, 2007; Raaijmakers, Posthumius, van Hout, van Engeland, & Matthys, 2011). The most commonly cited challenging behavior in young children include sleeping difficulties, mealtime and feeding issues, toilet training, temper tantrums, aggression, sibling rivalry and noncompliance (Campbell, 1995; Hale, Berger, LeBourgeois, & Brooks-Gunn, 2011; Lavigne et al.,

Correspondence concerning this article should be addressed to: Jillian L. Childres, PhD, NCSP; University of South Florida, Department of Pediatrics, Division of Neurobehavioral Health, 13101 N. Bruce B. Downs Blvd., Tampa, FL 33612. E-mail: jwillia6@health.usf.edu

1996). Higher rates of chronic behavior problems (25-35%) have been identified for children with risk factors, such as minority racial or ethnic group membership (Choi & Jackson, 2011; Copage, Bennett, & McNeil, 2001) or low-socioeconomic status (Gross et al., 2003; Webster-Stratton, 1998; Zhai, Brooks-Gunn, & Wald-fogel, 2011).

The impact of challenging behavior in young children has been well-documented and in general, the earlier the age of onset, the more stable and in-tense the associated outcomes will be (Dishion, French, & Patterson, 1995; McCrae, 2009; Meisch & Wesbrook, 2011). Behavior problems which emerge in the toddler or preschool years have been shown to predict childhood academic failure, social isolation, adolescent delinquency and gang membership, and adult incarceration (Dishion, French, & Patterson). As the prevalence rates of challenging behavior among young children continue to rise, professionals across disciplines have de-veloped a variety of interventions to help prevent and treat these behaviors. Group-delivered behavioral parent training has emerged as an economical and effective intervention that empowers parents to prevent and address challenging behavior in young children (Lundahl, Risser, & Lovejoy, 2006; Maughan, Christiansen, Jenson, Olympia, & Clark, 2005; Nelson, 1995; Sandall & Ostrosky, 1999; Smith & Fox, 2003). *Helping Our Toddlers, Developing Our Children's Skills* (HOT DOCS; Armstrong, Lilly, & Curtiss, 2006a, 2006b) is a group-delivered behavioral parent training program, which has recently been shown to result in positive outcomes for participants (Armstrong, Hornbeck, Beam, Mack, & Popkave, 2006; Salinas, Smith, & Armstrong, 2011; Williams, 2007, 2009; Williams, Armstrong, Agazzi, & Bradley-Klug, 2010).

Despite early findings supporting the positive outcomes of the HOT DOCS program, previous evaluations of this curriculum have lacked the rigorous meth-odology of a controlled trial necessary to consider the program as an evidence-based intervention. The current research project is a pilot study evaluation using a waitlist-control design to evaluate the effectiveness of the HOT DOCS program. The specific aims of the study were to evaluate the effectiveness of the HOT DOCS parent training program in:

1. Reducing caregivers' perceptions of the severity of children's problem behaviors;
2. Increasing participants' knowledge of child development and behavioral principles; and
3. Decreasing participants' stress associated with providing care to young children.

Method

Intervention Program

HOT DOCS, or *Helping Our Toddlers Developing Our Children's Skills* (Armstrong, Lilly, & Curtiss, 2006a) is a behavioral parent training program that incorporates both behavioral and ecological perspectives in its theoretical framework. HOT DOCS was designed to teach caregivers a problem-solving process based upon the foundation of behavioral principles (e.g., antecedents, consequences, and function of behavior) delivered in parent-friendly language. Unlike other parent training programs that focus on teaching parents to eliminate specific behavior problems, HOT DOCS empowers caregivers to use a step-by-step method to identify features of the environment and interpersonal interactions that may contribute to the reinforcement or maintenance of current and future problem behaviors. HOT DOCS is unique in that the same curriculum is used to train parents, other caregivers, and child service professionals all in the same group at the same time. This allows parents to bring their support network with them to classes enhancing the consistency of skill implementation across caregivers and across settings outside of the training session. Other programs such as Incredible Years (Webster-Stratton, 1998) and Triple P-Positive Parenting Practices (Sanders, 1999) have separate curricula for parents, children, teachers, and caregivers.

HOT DOCS is delivered over six consecutive weekly sessions of 2 hours each for a total of 12 hours of classroom-based instruction. The HOT DOCS program is in its fourth year of implementation, but no comprehensive study of the impact of the intervention on caregivers' knowledge and perceptions of target children's behavior has been undertaken and no comparisons between participants in this program and those receiving no treatment (e.g., control group) or an alternative treatment (e.g., direct therapy with the child) has been conducted.

Participants

We recruited parents and caregivers of young children (ages 17 months - 8 years) with challenging behavior through community advertisements (e.g., posters, brochures, fliers posted in community locations such as libraries, daycare facilities, and churches) and through clinical referrals by providing information about the program to local pediatricians and child service providers. As caregivers registered, they were placed on a waitlist for upcoming classes. In March of 2009, there were 233 caregivers on the waitlist. The first 75 caregivers on the list, as determined by date of registration, were assigned to the treatment condition, and the remaining 158 caregivers were assigned to the waitlist-control condition.

The 75 caregivers in the treatment condition were contacted by phone and mail and invited to attend the HOT DOCS sessions beginning in April of 2009. Of the original 75 caregivers, 10 declined to participate due to scheduling conflicts (e.g., work or school commitments) or because they had found alternative intervention services for their child (e.g., speech therapy, individual counseling). Of the 65 caregivers who committed to attending the classes, 59 caregivers attended at least the first session of treatment. Of these participants, 47 completed pre- and post-test data.

We contacted the 158 caregivers in the waitlist condition by phone and mail and invited them to participate in a waitlist-control group activity. We informed caregivers that we wanted to study the effectiveness of HOT DOCS by collecting information from them while they waited for treatment and then compare their data to caregivers currently attending classes. We assured them that they would not be penalized for declining to participate and would still be invited to attend the next available HOT DOCS classes. However, as an incentive for participation, we told them that if they consented to participate in the waitlist-control group they would be moved to the top of the waitlist for the next available classes, which could possibly shorten the time they would have to wait to attend classes. Of the 158 caregivers in the waitlist-control condition, 69 consented to participation. We collected pre- and post-test data from 53 participants.

Demographic information was compared across the treatment and waitlist-control groups (see Table 1). Caregivers in both conditions were similar with respect to age (19-62 yrs, $M = 35.14$, $SD = 7.81$), gender, relationship to target child, marital status, and education level. The groups differed significantly in terms of caregiver's ethnicity, $t (108) = 3.418$, $p < .05$, with the treatment group having more Hispanic or Latino caregivers (39.0%) than the waitlist-control group (18.8%) and the waitlist-control group not having any Asian, Native American, or Other/Mixed caregivers. As a group, the majority of caregivers was white (47.7%), married (59.4%), and mothers (76.6% female, 84.4% biological parents). Many had a 4-year college or graduate degree (42.2%). Both groups of caregivers had similar scores on pre-test measures, including knowledge of child development and behavior, perceived stress, and ratings of the severity of their child's problem behaviors. At pre-test, both groups of caregivers reported that their children's be-havior was well below a clinical level of significance as measured by the Child Behavior Checklist (CBCL; Achenbach, 2001). This is likely due to the recruiting and enrollment procedures unique to this parenting program, in that all parents who are interested in attending can register and attend the classes. Participation in the program is not restricted to caregivers of only those children who have been diagnosed with a behavioral or medical condition, but is open to all caregivers struggling to manage challenging behavior.

Overall, target children ranged in age from 17 months to 8 years of age ($M = 43.78$ months, $SD = 18.61$). Target children in both the treatment and waitlist-con-trol groups were similar with respect to age, gender, preexisting diagnosis, type of medical insurance, current services or therapies, and type of school or daycare (see

Table 2). There were more boys (65.6%) than girls in the sample and the majority of target children were reported to have a preexisting diagnosis (57.8%). Of those who had preexisting diagnoses, most had a diagnosis of speech/language impairment (29.7%) or autism spectrum disorder, ASD (18.0%). Other preexisting diagnoses reported by caregivers included global developmental delays (17.2%), medical/genetic conditions (13.3%), and behavioral/psychological disorders (10.9%).

Measures

HOT DOCS Demographics Form. The Demographics Form was developed by the HOT DOCS authors in order to collect standardized information about the participants and children (Armstrong, Curtiss, & Lilly, 2006). This form includes 10 questions requesting participants' gender and age, target child's age, age(s) of other children in the home, type and name of health insurance, participants' relationship to targeted child, ethnicity, and level of education.

HOT DOCS Knowledge Test. The Knowledge Test was also developed by the HOT DOCS authors in order to assess participants' verbal knowledge of child development, behavioral principles, and parenting strategies prior to and subsequent to participation in HOT DOCS classes (Armstrong, Curtiss, & Lilly, 2006). The test consists of 20 "True/False" statements and takes approximately 10 minutes to complete. Content validity rests on the assumption that test items were drawn from principles in texts and scholarly articles on child development, behaviorism, and child rearing which represent the knowledge required of persons who work with young children and especially those with challenging behavior. All of the principles covered in HOT DOCS could not be represented in a 20 item test but the principal investigator did review the items to ensure key principles were included. For the purposes of this study, only total scores were recorded and analyzed. Total scores were computed by coding each correct response as a "1" and each incorrect response as a "0" and summing the total points for each participant. Cronbach's measure of internal consistency reliability was calculated (α = .47) and suggested that 47% of the total score variance was due to true score variance.

The instrument was developed by HOT DOCS staff, including Ph.D. level psychologists and doctoral level school psychology students all of whom have expertise in child development, parent education and behavioral modification. The items were evaluated for clarity and how well each question was linked to the objectives of the curriculum (e.g., curricular validity). Further, after the test was implemented with three cohorts of HOT DOCS participants, its instructional validity was evaluated by reviewing the scripted notes in the trainer's manual and determining if the notes included instruction on the specific content measured by items on the test.

Table 1

Demographic Characteristics of Caregivers

Characteristic	HOT DOCS ($n = 59$)	Control ($n = 69$)	Overall ($N = 128$)
Age (19-62 yrs) [M (SD)]	35.13 (7.81)	35.15 (10.38)	35.14 (9.11)
Gender [number (%)]			
Female	44 (74.6)	54 (78.3)	98 (76.6)
Male	15 (25.4)	15 (21.7)	30 (23.4)
Relationship [n (%)]			
Biological parent	51 (86.4)	57 (82.6)	108 (84.4)
Adoptive parent	3 (5.1)	1 (1.4)	4 (3.1)
Grandparent	1 (1.7)	7 (10.1)	8 (6.3)
Other	4 (6.8)	4 (5.7)	8 (6.2)
Marital Status [n (%)]			
Married	36 (61.0)	40 (58.0)	76 (59.4)
Single	7 (11.9)	10 (14.5)	17 (13.3)
Divorced	1 (1.7)	7 (10.1)	8 (6.3)
Separated	2 (3.4)	1 (1.4)	3 (2.3)
Other	2 (3.4)	2 (2.9)	4 (3.1)
Not Reported	11 (18.6)	9 (13.0)	20 (15.6)
Ethnicity [n (%)]			
White	26 (44.1)	35 (50.7)	61 (47.7)
Hispanic or Latino	23 (39.0)	13 (18.8)	36 (28.1)
Black/African American	2 (3.4)	6 (8.7)	8 (6.3)
Native American	3 (5.1)	--	3 (2.3)
Asian	1 (1.7)	--	1 (0.8)
Other/Mixed	1 (1.7)	--	1 (0.8)
Not Reported	3 (5.1)	15 (21.7)	18 (14.1)
Education [n (%)]			
Less than High School	5 (8.5)	3 (4.3)	8 (6.3)
High School	12 (20.3)	20 (29.0)	32 (25.0)
Some college or training	9 (15.3)	7 (10.1)	16 (12.6)

Characteristic	HOT DOCS ($n = 59$)	Control ($n = 69$)	Overall ($N = 128$)
4-Year or Graduate Degree	29 (49.1)	25 (36.2)	54 (42.2)
Not Reported	4 (6.8)	14 (20.3)	18 (14.1)

Note. CBCL = Child Behavior Checklist. Based on a series of independent means *t*-tests, groups did not differ significantly in any demographic category with the exception of Ethnicity, t (108) = 3.418, $p < .05$.

Behavior Rating Scales. The Child Behavior Checklist (CBCL; Achenbach, 2001) was developed to assess childhood behavior problems. There are multiple versions of the CBCL that are used depending on the child's age and the source of information. The CBCL 1½-5 was developed for use with children between the ages of 18 and 71 months of age and can be completed by parents/caregivers and/or teachers/caregivers. All versions of the CBCL are available in English and Spanish.

The CBCL 6-18 was developed for use with children and adolescents between the ages of 6 years and 18 years-11 months of age and can be completed by parents/caregivers, teachers, or as a self-report scale. The CBCL 1½ -5 and 6-18 each report problem behavior scores grouped into two broad-band factors (internalizing and externalizing problems), a total broad-band score derived by averaging weighted scores from the broad-band factors, and eight narrow-band subscales. Scores are expressed as T-scores with a mean of 50 and a standard deviation of 10.

A T-score of 64 or below is in the normal range; 65-69 is in the borderline range; and 70 or above is in the clinical range. Scores in the borderline or clinical range indicate that a child's behavior problems are more significant than other children the same age and gender. The CBCL manual (Achenbach, 2001) reports median internal consistency coefficients for the Internalizing and Externalizing scales that range from .76 to .92. Studies of the CBCL subscales indicated high retest reliability ($r = .89$) and adequate interrater reliability ($r = .66$). CBCL rating scales were completed at the first session and again six to eight weeks post-training at the booster session.

HOT DOCS Program Evaluation Survey. The Program Evaluation Survey was developed by the HOT DOCS authors to assess participants' perceptions of the effectiveness of the parent training program (Armstrong, Curtiss, & Lilly, 2006). The survey consists of eight statements about the benefits of HOT DOCS to participants, the teaching skills of HOT DOCS trainers, and the impact of the program on child and family behaviors and relationships. Participants were asked to respond on a 4-point Likert scale as "Strongly Agree," "Agree," "Disagree," or "Strongly Disagree." The survey also consists of five questions with response options provided, which prompted participants to share their perceptions on the usefulness of the program as well as any suggestions for future trainings or improvements to

Table 2

Demographic Characteristics of Target Children

Characteristic	HOT DOCS (*n* = 59)	Control (*n* = 69)	Overall (*N* = 128)
Age (17-96 mos) [*M* (*SD*)]	43.78 (18.61)	41.76 (16.63)	42.71 (17.54)
Gender [number (%)]			
Female	19 (32.2)	25 (36.2)	44 (34.4)
Male	40 (67.8)	44 (63.8)	84 (65.6)
Existing Diagnosis[a] [*n* (%)]			
None	24 (40.7)	30 (43.4)	54 (42.2)
Autism spectrum disorder	11 (18.6)	12 (17.4)	23 (18.0)
Speech/Language	15 (25.4)	23 (33.3)	38 (29.7)
Developmental Delay	8 (13.6)	14 (20.3)	22 (17.2)
Behavior/Psychological	8 (13.6)	6 (8.7)	14 (10.9)
Medical/Genetic	6 (10.2)	11 (15.9)	17 (13.3)
Type of Insurance [n (%)]			
Private	32 (54.2)	27 (39.1)	59 (46.1)
Medicaid	19 (32.2)	20 (29.0)	39 (30.5)
None	4 (6.8)	--	4 (3.1)
Not Reported	4 (6.8)	22 (31.9)	26 (20.3)
Current Therapy Services[b] [*n* (%)]			
None	21 (35.6)	21 (30.4)	42 (32.8)
Speech Therapy	9 (15.3)	28 (40.6)	37 (28.9)
Physical Therapy	--	3 (4.3)	3 (2.3)
Occupational Therapy	1 (1.7)	5 (7.2)	6 (4.7)
Special Education	2 (3.4)	4 (5.8)	6 (4.7)
Early Intervention	--	8 (11.6)	8 (6.3)
Individual Counseling	2 (3.4)	--	2 (1.6)
Group Counseling	--	1 (1.4)	1 (0.8)
Not Reported	26 (44.1)	15 (21.7)	41 (32.0)
Type of School/Daycare[c] [*n* (%)]			
Home w/parent or relative	15 (25.4)	18 (26.1)	33(25.8)
Daycare w/friend or relative	--	5 (7.2)	5 (3.9)

Characteristic	HOT DOCS	Control	Overall
	(n = 59)	(n = 69)	(N = 128)
Daycare professional	7 (11.9)	16 (23.2)	23 (18.0)
Preschool	7 (11.9)	12 (17.4)	19 (14.8)
Voluntary Pre-Kindergarten	2 (3.4)	2 (2.9)	4 (3.1)
Elementary School	3 (5.1)	5 (7.2)	8 (6.3)
Not Reported	26 (44.1)	15 (21.7)	41 (32.0)

Note. Based on a series of independent means *t*-tests, groups did not differ significantly in any demographic category.

ᵃSome children had more than one preexisting diagnosis.

ᵇSome children had more than one current therapy.

ᶜSome children had more than one type of school or daycare.

the current program. Information about reliability and validity were not available for this instrument.

Perceived Stress Scale. The Perceived Stress Scale-10 Items (PSS-10, Cohen & Williamson, 1988) is a brief, self-report measure of the degree to which one's life activities and experiences are perceived as stressful. The scale was normed on a large, varied national sample ($N = 2,387$) and has been shown to have good reliability ($\alpha = .78$) and "moderate validity" (Cohen & Williamson, 1988, p. 55). Scores on the PSS-10 are obtained by summing the participants' responses across all items. Item numbers four, five, seven, and eight are reverse-scored ($4 = 0, 3 = 1, 2 = 2, 1 = 3$) and included in the participants total score. Higher scores on the PSS suggest greater levels of overall perceived stress and lower scores represent lower levels of perceived stress. Average scores obtained for the normative sample ranged from 11.9 to 14.7 with a mean score of 12.9.

Group Assignment

This study included caregivers of children with early emerging challenging behavior using a waitlist-control group design with two conditions (HOT DOCS and waitlist-control) and measures at two points in time (pre- and post-intervention). A pragmatic waitlist-control group design was applied in this study. The demand for the HOT DOCS program outpaces the program's capacity to deliver the intervention, resulting in a time delay between when caregivers register for the program and when they begin attending sessions. Participants were assigned to the treatment or waitlist groups on the basis of their time of registration. The program serves a maximum of 65 caregivers at one time. To account for attrition, the first

75 caregivers on the registration list were assigned to the treatment group and the remaining participants were assigned to the waitlist group. Participants were not randomly assigned to treatment or control groups.

Procedure

The HOT DOCS program was provided at a university-based child development clinic. Assessments were conducted by mail for the waitlist-control group and in the clinic during sessions for the treatment group. Assessment data were collected at three times, pre-test (class 1), post-test (class 6), and follow-up (2 months after class 6). Caregivers in the waitlist-control group were mailed assessments at the same time the treatment group was administered the assessments.

The HOT DOCS group was delivered over 6 consecutive weeks. Four cohorts of caregivers attended sessions once a week. Three of the classes were delivered in English and one class was delivered in Spanish. All curriculum materials have been translated to Spanish and culturally adapted to Hispanic/Latino families (Agazzi et al., 2010).

We collected demographic information, knowledge of child development and behavior management (at pre- and post-test), structured behavior rating scales, and social validity and acceptability measures. The Demographics Form and the Knowledge Pretest were completed by participants during the first session. Behavior rating scales were completed on each child and returned by the second session. Participants completed the Knowledge Post-test during the final session of training. Two months after the final session caregivers were mailed a post-test behavior rating scale and a postage-paid return envelope.

Treatment Fidelity

HOT DOCS groups were delivered by experienced and proficient trainers who had been teaching the program for a minimum of 3 years. Trainers delivered the program as scripted in the program manual and by using the standardized presentations. HOT DOCS maintains implementation fidelity by providing all course materials, including participant manuals, as a comprehensive training curriculum. The materials include a progressive muscle relaxation CD, supplementary handouts, toys for homework activities, raffle prizes to encourage data completion, and reminder notes about missing data. Trainers are certified to deliver the curriculum following successful completion of a training workshop in the HOT DOCS program and satisfactory evaluations on their co-teaching performance by an experienced trainer. Other methods of ensuring treatment fidelity include formative evaluation using data from participant-completed satisfaction questionnaires and trainer feedback to the authors.

Results

Attrition

Attrition rates were similar to those found in previous studies of this treatment program (Agazzi et al., 2010; Williams, 2007, 2009; Williams et al., 2010), averaging approximately 22% across treatment and waitlist-control groups. At post-test (class 6), 12 caregivers from the treatment group did not complete assessments, while 16 caregivers from the waitlist-control group did not complete assessments. As with previous evaluations of the HOT DOCS program, much higher rates of attrition were found with the follow-up assessments administered 2 months after the intervention ended, averaging 49% across treatment and waitlist-control groups. At follow-up, 40 caregivers from the treatment group did not return the assessments, while 23 caregivers in the waitlist-control group did not return the assessments.

A series of *t*-tests compared those with complete data sets ("completers") to those participants who either dropped out before completion of the program or who did not turn in post-test measures across both the treatment and waitlist control groups. No significant differences were found between completers and non-completers on any of the demographic variables with the exception of caregivers' race/ethnicity. In further study of the race/ethnicity frequencies reported by completers and non-completers, data indicated that the difference between the two groups was in the number of participants with missing race/ethnicity information (e.g., participants who left that item blank on the demographics form).

Attendance

Participants in the treatment group attended an average of 4.42 ($SD = 4.67$) of the 6 total sessions. Within the treatment condition, 59 out of 65 (91%) participants attended at least one session, and the majority of participants (79%) attended four or more sessions.

Preliminary Analyses (Equivalence)

There were no significant differences between the treatment and waitlist-control groups in participant knowledge or caregivers' ratings of children's problem behavior at pre-test. Participants in both groups rated their children's problem behavior as being more severe and problematic than expected in a normal distribution. This finding was expected, as caregivers are referred or self-refer to the program because their children are demonstrating early emerging challenging behavior.

Caregivers' Perception of Child Problem Behavior

As shown in Figure 1, caregivers in the treatment condition rated the severity of their child's problem behavior an average of 6.08 points lower at post-test (M = 51.31, SD = 11.21) than they did at pre-test (M = 57.39, SD = 11.42). Caregivers in the waitlist-control condition rated the severity of their child's behavior an average of 2.72 point higher at post-test (M = 60.26, SD = 11.30) than they did at pre-test (M = 57.54, SD = 12.47). On the CBCL, higher scores indicate more severe levels of problem behavior. Therefore, a decrease in scores from pre-test to post-test indicates caregivers in the treatment group perceived their target child to have significantly less severe levels of problem behavior following participation in the program while participants in the waitlist-control group perceived their target child's problem behavior to have become more severe. Refer to Table 3 for group means and sample sizes at pre- and post-test times.

Results of a repeated measures ANOVA indicated that the differential ratings of the change in child behavior were significantly different for participants in the treatment and waitlist-control groups, $F(1,56) = 16.88$, $p < .001$, $\eta^2 = .232$. Partial

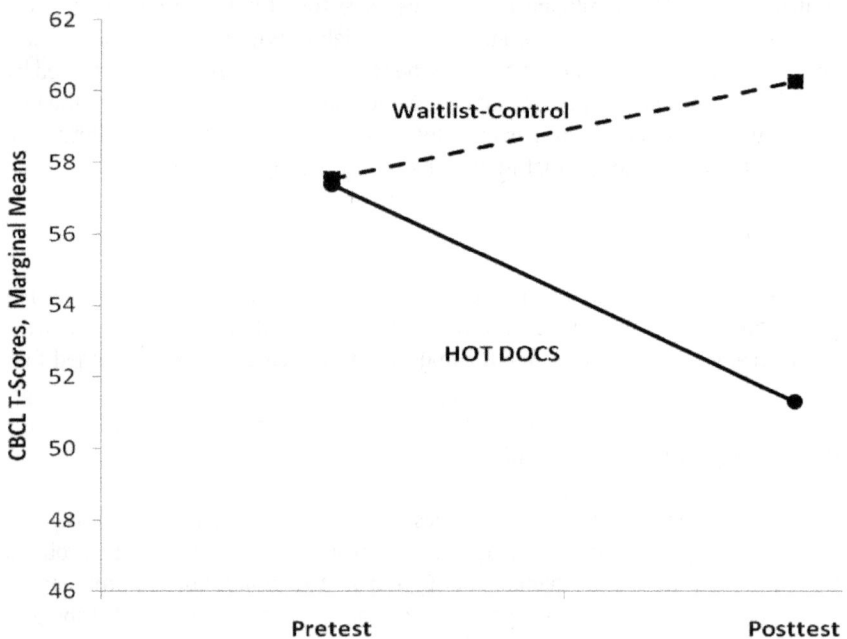

Figure 1. Pre- and post-test CBCL T-scores for participants in the waitlist-control and HOT DOCS groups.

Table 3

Outcome Variables at Pre- and Post-Test

	HOT DOCS		Waitlist-Control	
Measure	Pre	Post	Pre	Post
CBCL Internalizing[a]				
Mean	56.52	51.31	56.68	59.88
Standard deviation	11.99	12.45	13.04	10.99
N	54	16	66	43
CBCL Externalizing				
Mean	58.26	51.31	58.39	60.63
Standard deviation	10.84	9.97	11.89	11.61
N	54	16	66	43
CBCL Marginal Means[b]				
Mean	57.39	51.31	57.54	60.26
Standard deviation	11.42	11.21	12.47	11.30
N	54	16	66	43
Knowledge Test[c]				
Mean	15.69	17.00	15.99	15.79
Standard deviation	2.22	2.01	2.00	2.53
N	59	47	69	53
Perceived Stress[d]				
Mean	18.29	18.91	19.72	22.41
Standard deviation	5.93	6.35	7.03	6.16
N	58	45	69	41

[a]CBCL Scales: <64 = Non-significant, 65-70 = Borderline, >70 = Clinically Significant.
[b]Marginal Means: average of Internalizing and Externalizing scores.
[c]Knowledge Test: 20 True/False items, 1 = each correct answer.
[d]Perceived Stress Scale: 0-40, mean = 12.9, lower scores indicate less perceived stress.

eta-squared (η^2) values are used as estimates of effect size. Partial η^2 values range from 0 to 1 and indicate the proportion of variance in the dependent variable that can be accounted for by the independent variable (Trusty, Thompson, & Petrocelli, 2004). A partial η^2 value of .232 for the interaction effect indicates that 23.2% of the variance in the difference in participants' ratings of children's behavior from pre-test to post-test can be accounted for by the group to which participants were assigned and the time of measurement. This value explains the impact of the statistically significant finding by comparing the amount of variance explained by the interaction between time and group assignment to the amount of variance explained by any of the variables individually or by chance alone (ranging from 0.0- 6.8%).

Caregiver Knowledge

As shown in Figure 2, caregivers in the treatment condition scored an average of 1.31 points higher on the knowledge test given after participating in the program (M = 17.00, SD = 2.01) than they did before the program began (M = 15.69, SD = 2.22). Participants in the waitlist-control group scored an average of 0.20 points lower on the knowledge post-test (M = 15.79, SD = 2.53) than they did on the pre-test (M = 15.99, SD = 2.00).

Results of a repeated measures ANOVA indicated that the differences in knowledge from pre-test to post-test were significantly different for the treatment group and the waitlist-control group, $F(1, 98)$ = 10.92, p = .001, η^2 = .100. The interaction between group assignment and time of testing accounted for 10% of the variance in

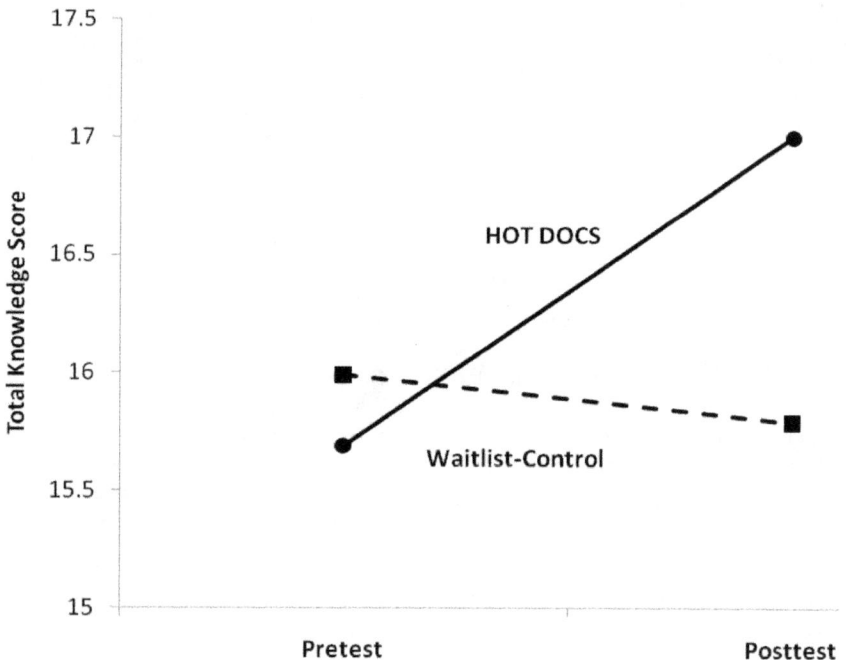

Figure 2. Pre- and post-test Knowledge scores for participants in the waitlist-control and HOT DOCS groups.

the change in participants' knowledge scores, as compared to variance accounted for by the individual variables or chance (1.7 - 4.2%).

Caregivers' Perceived Stress

As shown in Figure 3, caregivers in the treatment group perceived their stress at pre-test (M = 18.29, SD = 5.93) to be approximately the same at post-test (M = 18.91, SD = 6.35). Caregivers in the waitlist-control group also perceived their stress at pre-test (M = 19.72, SD = 7.03) to be relatively unchanged at post-test (M = 22.41, SD = 6.16). On the PSS higher ratings indicate more intense and negative perceptions of stress. Population estimates indicated that an average score on the PSS is 12.9 (Cohen & Williamson, 1988). Participants in this study indicated higher than average levels of perceived stress that remained stable from pre-test to post-test.

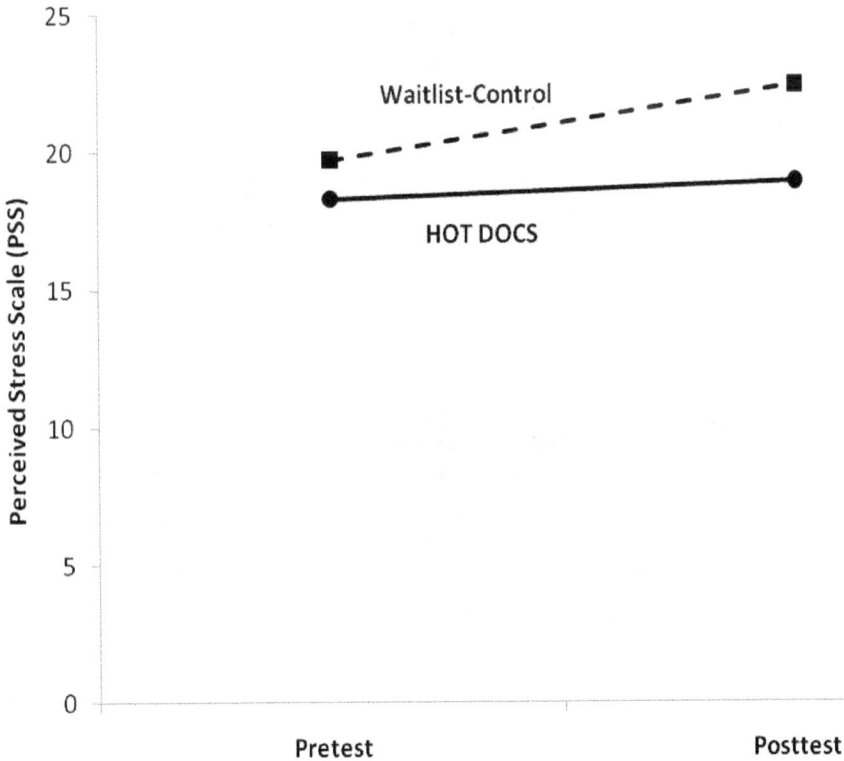

Figure 3. Pre- and post-test PSS scores for participants in the waitlist-control and HOT DOCS groups.

Discussion

Overall, results of this study indicate that the caregivers who received the intervention demonstrated significantly more positive outcomes than caregivers who did not receive the intervention. Improvements in the ratings of the severity of children's problem behaviors were significantly greater for participants assigned to the HOT DOCS group than for participants assigned to the waitlist-control group. Gains in caregivers' knowledge from pre-test to post-test were also significantly greater for treatment versus waitlist-control participants. Levels of perceived stress in caregivers did not significantly differ between the two groups. Participants in both conditions reported higher than average levels of stress at both pre-test and post-test times.

These findings suggest that the HOT DOCS parent training program is a successful method of early intervention for caregivers of young children with early emerging challenging behavior. The results enhance the developing evidence-base for the use of the HOT DOCS program with a varied population of caregivers of young children (Agazzi et al., 2010; Armstrong et al., 2006; Salinas et al., 2011; Williams, 2007, 2009; Williams et al., 2010). The results also augment the existing literature base supporting the use of group-delivered behavioral parent training as a method of preventing typically developing children with challenging behavior from developing clinically significant and/or diagnosable behavior disorders and as a method of intervention to address early emerging problem behaviors in young children (Lundahl et al., 2006; Maughan et al., 2005; Webster-Stratton, 1998).

Limitations

Several limitations associated with the study methodology and design are worthy of mention. First, as with previous studies of this intervention program (Agazzi et al., 2010; Williams, 2007; Williams, 2009), the return rate for post-test behavior rating scales in this pilot study was notably low (49%). Several methods have been implemented since the previous studies to increase the return rate, including the development of a booster session in which participants completed the rating scales in person and by offering incentives for returning the rating scales in the mail (e.g., gift cards, prizes). These modifications have resulted in measurable increases in the return rate for the overall sample from 28% to 49% over a 2-year period.

A second limitation is the method of participant assignment to the treatment and waitlist-control conditions. Participants were assigned based on a first-come, first-served basis, meaning that those participants at the top of the registration list were assigned to receive treatment first and the participants remaining on the registration list were assigned to the waitlist-control condition. Random assignment and matching based on demographic variables and pre-test measures would increase the strength of future studies of this program.

Third, the primary outcomes used in this study (CBCL, Knowledge Test, PSS) were indirect measures of caregiver and child behavior. Scores were based on caregiver reports of their own knowledge, skills, and emotions and their perceptions of children's behaviors. The findings would be strengthened by incorporating direct measures of caregiver and child behavior, such as coding of videotaped behaviors and interactions by an independent source. Finally, the follow-up measures were administered 8 weeks after completion of the program; thus, we cannot say that the gains were maintained beyond this point.

Future Directions

The findings from this study lead to several recommendations for future research. To overcome the methodological weaknesses in this study, another trial of this intervention should be done using a randomized controlled design with groups matched on demographic variables and/or scores on pre-test measures. Efforts should continue to be made to increase the return rate for post-test measures. To address the limitations created by the measurement instruments used in this study, future projects should incorporate direct measures of caregiver and child behavior; utilize the newly designed and validated multiple choice knowledge test (Agazzi & Childres, in preparation), which has demonstrated adequate levels of internal consistency and item discrimination; and consider developing a pre/post test that measures participants' ability to use the problem-solving chart in response to a video vignette or scenario. To further investigate the positive outcomes identified in this study, future research should include a follow-up component to explore the long-term maintenance of outcomes and skills learned in the intervention and whether or not these skills generalize across other caregivers and settings and lead to long-term benefits such as pro-social skills in the preschool classroom.

References

Achenbach, T. (2001). *Manual for the Achenbach system of empirically based assessment (ASEBA)*. Burlington, VT: University of Vermont, Research Center for Children, Youth, & Families.

Agazzi, H., & Childres, J. (In preparation). An instrument to assess caregiver knowledge of behavioral principles as applied to young children.

Agazzi, H., Salinas, A., Williams, J., Chiriboga, D., Ortiz, C., & Armstrong, K. (2010). Adaptation of a behavioral parent training curriculum for Hispanic caregivers: HOT DOCS Español. *Infant Mental Health Journal*, 32, 182-200.

Armstrong, K., Hornbeck, M., Beam, B., Mack, K., & Popkave, K. (2006). Evaluation of a curriculum for caregivers of young children with challenging behaviors. *Journal of Early Childhood and Infant Psychology*, 2, 51-61.

Armstrong, K., Lilly, C., & Curtiss, H. (2006a). *Helping our toddlers developing our children's skills*. Tampa, FL: University of South Florida, Department of Pediatrics, Division of Child Development.

Armstrong, K., Lilly, C., & Curtiss, H. (2006b). *Helping our toddlers developing our children's skills: En Espanol*. Tampa, FL: University of South Florida, Department of Pediatrics, Division of Child Development.

Campbell, S. (1995). Behavior problems in preschool children: A review of recent research. *Journal of Child Psychology & Psychiatry & Allied Disciplines*, 36, 113-149.

Choi, J., & Jackson, A. (2011). Fathers' involvement and child behavior problems in poor African American single mother families. *Children and Youth Services Review, 33(5)*, 698-704.

Cohen, S., & Williamson, G. (1988). Perceived stress in a probability sample of the United States. In S. Spacapan & S. Oskamp (Eds.), *The Social Psychology of Health* (pp. 31-67). Newbury Park, CA: Sage.

Copage, L., Bennett, G., & McNeil, C. (2001). A comparison between African American and Caucasian children referred for treatment of behavior problems. *Child and Family Behavior Therapy*, 23, 1–14.

Dishion, T., French, D., & Patterson, G. (1995). The developmental and ecology of antisocial behavior. In D. Cicchetti & D. J. Cohen (Eds.), *Developmental Psychopathology, Vol. 2: Risk, disorder, and adaptation* (pp. 421-471). New York: John Wiley & Sons.

Gross, D., Fogg, L., Webster-Stratton, C., Garvey, C., Julion, W., & Grady, J. (2003). Parent training of toddlers in day care in low-income urban communities. *Journal of Consulting & Clinical Psychology, 71*, 261-278.

Hale, L., Berger, L., LeBourgeois, M., & Brooks-Gunn, J. (2011). A longitudinal study of preschoolers' language-based bedtime routines, sleep duration, and well-being. *Journal of Family Psychology, 25(3)*, 423-433.

Knapp, P., Ammen, S., Arstein-Kerslake, C., Poulsen, M., & Mastergeorge, A. (2007). Feasibility of expanding services for very young children in the public mental health setting. *Journal of the American Academy of Child and Adolescent Psychiatry, 46*, 152-161.

Lavigne, J., Gibbons, R., Christoffel, K. K., Arend, R., Rosenbaum, D., Binns, H., ... Isaacs, C. (1996). Prevalence rates and correlates of psychiatric disorders among preschool children. *Journal of the American Academy of Child & Adolescent Psychiatry, 35*, 204-214.

Lundahl, B., Risser, H., & Lovejoy, C. (2006). A meta-analysis of parent training: Moderators and follow-up effects. *Clinical Psychology Review, 26*, 86-104.

Maughan, D., Christiansen, E., Jenson, W., Olympia, D., & Clark, E. (2005). Behavioral parent training as a treatment for externalizing behaviors and disruptive behavior disorders: A meta-analysis. *School Psychology Review, 34*, 267-286.

McCrae, J. (2009). Emotional and behavioral problems reported in child welfare over 3 years. *Journal of Emotional and Behavioral Disorders, 17*(1), 17-28.

Meisch, A. D., & Westbrook, T. R. (2011). Family risks and protective factors Pathways to Early Head Start toddlers'social-emotional functioning. *Early Childhood Research Quarterly, 26*(1), 74-86.

Nelson, C. (1995). A meta-analysis of parent education programs for children two to nine years. *Dissertation Abstracts International: Section B: The Sciences and Engineering, 56*, 1686.

Raaijmakers, M., Posthumius, J., van Hout, B., van Engeland, H., & Matthys, W. (2011). Cross-sectional study into the costs and impact on family functioning of 4-year-old children with aggressive behavior. *Prevention Science, 12*(2), 192-200.

Salinas, A., Smith, J., & Armstrong, K. (2011). Engaging fathers in behavioral parent training: Listening to fathers' voices. *Journal of Pediatric Nursing, 26*, 304-311.

Sandall, S., & Ostrosky, M. (Eds.). (1999). *Young exceptional children: Practical ideas for addressing challenging behaviors*. (1st Ed.). Denver: Division for Early Childhood of the Council for Exceptional Children.

Sanders, M. (1999). Triple P-positive parenting program: Towards an empirically validated multilevel parenting and family support strategy for the prevention of behavior and emotional problems in children. *Clinical Child and Family Psychology Review, 2*, 71-90.

Smith, B., & Fox, L. (2003, January). *Systems of Service Delivery: A Synthesis of Evidence Relevant to Young Children at Risk for or Who Have Challenging Behavior*. Retrieved September 21, 2006, from the Center for Evidence-Based Practice: Young Children with Challenging Behaviors website: http://challengingbehavior.fmhi.usf.edu/resources/smith-fox-jan03.pdf

Trusty, J., Thompson, B., & Petrocelli, J. (2004). Practical guide for reporting effect
    size in quantitative research in the Journal of Counseling & Development.
    Journal of Counseling & Development, 82, 107-110.
Webster-Stratton, C. (1998). Preventing conduct problems in Head Start children:
    Strengthening parenting competencies. *Journal of Consulting and Clinical
    Psychology, 66,* 715-730.
Williams, J. (2007). Caregivers' Perceptions of the Effectiveness of the *Helping
    Our Toddlers, Developing Our Children's Skills* Parent Training Program:
    A Pilot Study. *Psychological and Social Foundations.* Tampa, University of
    South Florida. Educational Specialist (EdS): 163.
Williams, J. (2009). *Helping our toddlers, developing our children's skills (HOT
    DOCS):* An Investigation of a parenting program to address challenging
    behavior in young children. *Psychological and Social Foundations.* Tampa,
    University of South Florida. Doctor of Philosophy (PhD): 217.
Williams, J., Armstrong, K., Agazzi, H., & Bradley-Klug, K. (2010). *Helping
    our toddlers, developing our children's skills (HOT DOCS): A parenting
    intervention to prevent and address challenging behavior in young children.*
    Manuscript submitted for publication.
Zhai, F., Brooks-Gunn, J., Waldfogel, J. (2011). Head Start and urban children's
    school readiness: A birth cohort study in 18 cities. *Developmental Psycho-
    logy, 47*(1), 134-152.

Development of the Quality of Life Questionnaire for Families of Young Children with Developmental Delays

Rachel Bowman
Duke University Medical Center

Joseph R. Scotti
West Virginia University

The present study describes the development of a quality of life questionnaire for use with families of young children (under 3 years of age) with developmental delays. Following a comprehensive review of the literature, we developed the Quality of Life Interview (QLI), which was subsequently piloted and reduced to a 28-item self-report questionnaire (Quality of Life Questionnaire for Families of Young Children with Developmental Delays; QLQ-FYCDD). A factor analysis resulted in four conceptually appealing factors (Developmental Level, Behavior Problem, Family Psychiatric History, Satisfaction/Support). Internal consistency among items was high and test-retest reliability ranged from acceptable to excellent on all subscales. Mothers of children with a developmental delay reported a lower quality of life (QLQ-FYCDD Total Score) than mothers of children with behavior problems; both groups reported a lower quality of life than mothers of children without a delay or behavior problems. Relations of scores to key demographic variables are presented, including racial/ethnic differences. Future uses for this psychometrically sound instrument are suggested.

Keywords: quality of life, children, families, developmental delay, early intervention.

Quality of life has emerged as an important area of research in psychological and medical arenas, yet little research has been conducted with very young children (under age 3 years) and families, particularly those with developmental delays and disabilities (Raat, Landgraf, Oostenbrink, Moll, & Essink-Bot, 2007; Wang et al., 2006). We provide an overview of the early intervention and quality of life literatures, and describe the development of a quality of life assessment tool that can be

Correspondence concerning this article should be addressed to: Rachel A. Bowman, PhD; Duke University Medical Center, Child Development and Behavioral Health Center; 402 Trent Drive #2906; Durham, NC 27705. E-mail: rachel.bowman@duke.edu.

utilized with families who have young children with developmental delays. There is debate about who can best assess quality of life in pediatric populations (i.e., self or others; Russell, Hudson, Long, & Phipps, 2006; Wang et al.); in the present study, the report of mothers was used due to the young age of the children involved.

Early intervention for the prevention and treatment of developmental delays and disabilities in children ages birth to three years is a critical area of programmatic development. When PL 101-476 [the Individuals with Disabilities Education Act (IDEA)], which established Part H (Infants and Toddlers with Disabilities Program of 1991), was passed, new and expanded services for infants and young children with developmental delays were created. The goals of early intervention are to improve the quality of life for the child and family, prevent developmental delay, ameliorate developmental delay in children with existing conditions (e.g., Down syndrome), and build on family and child skills through the provision of family-centered interventions (Brown & Brown, 1993; Wang et al., 2006). Although a key goal of early intervention, no psychometrically sound instruments exist to specifically assess quality life of families of young children with developmental delays.

There are well over 100 definitions of quality of life in the literature. Typically, quality of life is defined in terms of physical health, psychological well-being, happiness, self-esteem, social supports and relationships, financial resources, and life satisfaction (Cummins, McCabe, Romeo, & Gullone, 1994; Morrow, Quine, Heaton, & Craig, 2010; Young, Rice, Dixon-Woods, Colver, & Parkinson, 2007). For example, Schalock (1994) defined quality of life as a "concept that reflects a person's desired conditions of living related to home and community living, employment, and health functioning" (p.121). The most common factors assessed by quality of life instruments include home and community living, financial issues, health status, employment, possessions, social supports (e.g., family and friends), family and leisure activities, personal control, choices, and decision-making (Morrow et al.; Raat et al., 2007; Schalock; Young et al.). Consumer satisfaction with aspects such as housing, services, and employment has also been determined to be major indicators of quality of life (Leibowitz, McCalin, Evans, Ruma, & Rauner, 1994).

In the pediatric literature, several measures are available to assess quality of life in children with chronic illness or severe physical disabilities. Here, quality of life has typically been examined in terms of health-related quality of life, which refers to the "subjective and objective impact of dysfunction associated with an illness or injury, medical treatment, and health care policy" (Spieth & Harris, 1996, p. 177). Two types of quality of life measures have been reported in the literature. One type includes measures of generic health status; these are broadly applicable across types and severities of disease. The other type of measure is disease-specific, assessing concerns and issues of specific disease groups, such as cancer or asthma patients. An example of a generic measure is the Infant and Toddler Quality of Life Questionnaire, which was designed to assess health status and health-related quality of life for children 2 months to 5 years. Raat and colleagues

(2007) found this instrument to have adequate reliability and validity when used with very young children with and without respiratory disease. An example of a disease-specific assessment tool is the Pediatric Functional Assessment of Cancer Therapy - Childhood Brain Tumor Survivors. The questions address physical health, illness experiences, social and family issues, and survivor issues. A cross-cultural study supported the clinical utility of this tool in assessing quality of life issues for children and adolescents with regard to their general health and brain-tumor specific conditions (Yoo et al., 2010).

Developing methodologically sound quality of life assessment tools can be challenging. First, numerous definitions for quality of life exist (e.g., Green, Gardner, & Reid, 1997; Morrow et al., 2010; Schalock et al., 2002), despite some consensus among researchers regarding a common definition (Hall, Horner-Johnson, Krahn, & Lamb, 2011). A second challenge is related to how quality of life assessment tools are developed, with multiple published measures not including the procedural details of instrument development (e.g., Brotherson, Oakland, Secrist-Mertz, Litchfield, & Larson, 1995; Pedlar, Lord, & Van Loon, 1990; Robitail et al., 2007). Third, quality of life assessments are not routinely used by professionals because many measures lack reliability and validity (Nathan et al., 2004), and cultural relevance (Punpanich et al., 2010). With the increase in racial and ethnic diversity within service programs, researchers must include culturally diverse groups in their studies. Further, many instruments can be long and time-consuming to administer, particularly in clinical settings. Fourth, psychometric challenges present a methodological challenge. Specifically, there is disagreement about the use of test-retest reliability as a standard for judging quality of life instruments because changes in scores over time are *expected* with changes in aspects of quality of life (e.g., health status, finances, relationships; Morrow et al.; Spieth & Harris, 1996). However, test-retest reliability may be feasible within a short time span (such as one week), and measures of internal consistency can demonstrate other forms of reliability. Additionally, it can be difficult to distinguish between *random variation* and *true change* when dynamic states such as aspects of quality of life are assessed (Patrick & Deyo, 1989). Finally, how to compare clinically significant change at the individual level versus statistically significant group changes poses another methodological challenge (Morrow et al.).

Our goal with the present study was to develop and test a quality of life assessment tool for families with a child of three years or younger who has been diagnosed as having a developmental delay. In Phase I, we describe how the instrument was developed and piloted. In Phase II, we report on the administration of the instrument to a large sample to provide details of its psychometric properties.

Phase I: Item Development

Method

The purpose of the Phase I study was to develop a parent report form to assess the quality of life of families of young children with developmental delays. First, a literature review of quality of life research was conducted, and the Quality of Life Interview (QLI) was developed specifically for this study based on quality of life information and research in the developmental disabilities and pediatric psychology literature. Five professionals provided reviews and qualitative feedback regarding face and content validity of the several hundred potential interview items. Two of these professionals were doctoral-level faculty in a department of psychology, one was a doctoral candidate in clinical child psychology, and two held master's degrees in early childhood special education and developmental disabilities. Items were dropped, added, or revised based on clarity and content. The QLI contains 322 questions (not including demographic questions) and covers 11 quality of life domains: child and family-related services, housing, parental job issues, respite/daycare services, early intervention issues, relationships/social support, community activities, home activities, mealtime issues, child issues, and family issues.

Participants. The QLI was administered by the first author to 15 mothers who had children 3 years of age and under. The mothers were recruited through daycare and early intervention programs. Of the 15 mother/child pairs, 6 (40%) were white and 9 (60%) were black. Educational level of mothers ranged from less than high school to graduate school (87%, at least high school), and yearly income ranged from less than $3,000 to over $100,000 ($M = \$56,066$, $SD = \$91,014$, *Median* = $40,000). The population of the cities in which the families resided (Mothers provided city name, for which the authors obtained official population) ranged from 7,487 to 610,337 ($M = 238,858$, $SD = 286,845$, *Median* = 26,989), indicating a diversity of rural to urban settings (which may reflect access to services).

Child ages ranged from 3.5 to 36 months ($M = 23.8$ months, $SD = 12.3$). To cover a range of family situations that might differentially impact quality of life issues, we specifically recruited five mothers whose children had developmental delays[1] (Group DD), five whose children had behavior problems (Group BP) (i.e., no developmental delay, but problems that can impact quality of life), and five whose children did not exhibit a delay or behavior problem (Group TD). Of those five children with a developmental delay, three were born prematurely; the delays of the other two children were of uncertain origin. Of those children with a behavior problem, one was diagnosed with Attention Deficit/Hyperactivity Disorder; the other four children were not formally diagnosed but exhibited behavior problems

---

[1] For the purpose of this study, *developmental delay* refers to the Tennessee eligibility criteria in which a child is considered "delayed" if she/he has at least a 40% delay in one area of development and a 25% delay in two or more areas.

reported by daycare staff as significantly impacting learning and participation in center and home activities.

Procedures. Interviews were conducted in the mothers' homes or at a daycare center. Completion times ranged from 2 to 3 hours. Mothers were asked to first answer each question and to then rate its relevance to their family's quality of life, using a four-point rating scale (1 = *not at all relevant*, 4 = *highly relevant*). At the conclusion of the interview, the mothers were asked to suggest additional items that might be included.

Results

Item Analysis and Reduction. To reduce the QLI to a brief questionnaire, several procedures were utilized. First, 152 items were deleted as a result of at least one mother indicating the item as "not at all relevant." Second, mean scores for the relevance ratings of the 170 remaining items were reviewed (these ranged from a mean of 1.7 to 3.7). The 93 items with a mean relevance rating equal to or greater than 3.2 were retained[2]. Third, we evaluated these 93 items, intending to delete any with a skewed response distribution; all items were retained as none showed evidence of statistically significant skew. Fourth, questions that were similar in content, were less clearly worded, or had a *yes/no* format were dropped. This four-step process resulted in 58 (of 322) items being retained for Phase II.

Phase II: Internal Consistency, Reliability, and Initial Validity

Method

Participants. The 58-item version of the Quality of Life Questionnaire for Families of Young Children with Developmental Delays (QLQ-FYCDD, or QLQ for short) was administered to 228 mothers of young children three years of age and younger. As in Phase I, mothers whose children met the criteria for a developmental delay (Group DD), behavior problems (Group BP), and typical development (Group TD) were recruited. Recruitment occurred through early intervention centers, daycare centers, preschools, churches, and Mothers' Day Out programs in Tennessee, Arkansas, Virginia, and West Virginia.

Procedures. To recruit mothers, advertisements were distributed through agency directors, and talks were given to parent groups at agency functions (e.g., parent support group, parent visitation night). The QLQ was distributed to interested mothers either directly or by agency staff. Completed questionnaires were

---

[2]   The score of 3.2 represents 80% of the range between the lowest and highest mean relevance ratings. We selected this value in accord with the multiple considerations for demonstrating content validity as discussed by Nunnally and Bernstein (1994); that is, identifying those items judged by the participating mothers as being the most relevant to their quality of life (i.e., the top 20% of the range).

either collected by agency directors and mailed to the investigators, or they were mailed back directly by the mothers using self-addressed, stamped envelopes that were provided. Mothers received $5 compensation for participation.

A subsample of 34 mothers (15 each from Groups TD and DD; 4 from Group BP) agreed to complete the QLQ twice. We attempted to randomly select these test-retest participants. However, due to an understandable lack of interest in completing the QLQ twice, participants were asked directly if they would volunteer for this portion of the study. Mothers willing to participate in the retest completed a second QLQ an average of 8.2 days later (SD = 2.9; range = 3 to 19 days). The retest period of approximately one week was chosen as quality of life aspects are dynamic and significant changes can occur over relatively short periods of time. This retest period was also consistent with several other quality of life studies (French, Christie, & Snowden, 1994; Moos & Moos, 1981).

Results

Our purpose in conducting the Phase II study was to determine the reliability (internal consistency, test-retest) of the QLQ, to determine validity (i.e., group differences), and to provide some initial descriptive findings. The demographic data are presented in Table 1, by group. Mother/child race/ethnicity did not differ by group, with 67% of the sample being White, 26% Black, and 5% Bi-racial, with 1% each for Asian, Hispanic, and Other. The overall mean child age was 21.7 months (SD = 10.1), with children in Group TD being significantly younger than in the other two groups, $F(2, 221)$ = 8.7, $p < .001$; Tukey's Least Significant Difference Test (LSD) for post hoc comparisons, $p < .01$. Overall, 43.4% of the children were female, with somewhat fewer females in Group DD and somewhat more in the Group BP, as compared to Group TD, $X^2(2)$ = 6.1, $p < .05$. The most common diagnoses for Group DD children included developmental delay, speech/language disorder, Down syndrome, and autism spectrum disorders, respectively. Mothers reported whether their child engaged in each of eight categories of behavior problems (tantrums, mealtime, bedtime, aggression, noncompliance, property destruction, self-injury, anxiety/fears). The three groups significantly differed from each other in the total number of behavior problems reported, $F(2, 225)$ = 40.2, $p < .001$; $LSD, p < .001$, consistent with group membership (Group BP > Group DD > Group TD).

Mothers averaged 28.3 years of age (SD = 6.4), with no group differences; however, mothers in Group DD reported having more children than mothers in the other groups, $F(2, 217)$ = 7.5, $p < .001$; LSD, $p < .01$. Over 90% of mothers had completed at least high school and 36% had completed a college degree or higher; family annual income averaged $50,159 ($SD$ = $46,263). There were no group differences for education and income (28%, unrelated to group, did not report income). Thirty-two percent of the mothers resided in a city with a population exceeding 100,000; 45% lived in a town of under 10,000 persons. These numbers indicate

Table 1

Demographic Variables by Group for Phase II Study

Variable	Typical Development (*n* = 102)	Behavior Problem (*n* = 43)	Developmental Delay (*n* = 83)
Mother/child race/ethnicity			
White	72%	53%	67%
Black	21%	42%	24%
Other	7%	5%	9%
Child age (months)	18.8 (10.0)	25.4 (10.1)	23.4 (9.4)
Child gender (% female)	47.5%	53.5%	32.9%
Total number of behavior problems	2.4 (1.5)	5.1 (1.8)	3.8 (2.1)
Mother age (years)	27.9 (6.1)	27.0 (5.7)	29.6 (6.8)
Number of children	1.8 (1.1)	1.8 (0.8)	2.4 (1.4)
Mother's education			
Less than high school	8%	14%	9%
Completed college	38%	26%	41%
Yearly family income	$52,848 ($36,858)	$38,321 ($31,397)	$53,405 ($59,448)
Population where reside	123,691 (229,021)	206,477 (284,137)	310,706 (298,831)

Note. Values are means (standard deviations) unless otherwise indicated.

geographic diversity (rural to urban), with a possible relation to need for special services as the population of the city of residence was larger for Group DD than the other two groups, $F(2, 225) = 11.2, p < .001$; LSD, $p < .05$.

Item reduction. The 58 items of the QLQ were examined for missing values (less than 1% missing, these were replaced by the modal group value for the item) and variance (two items were dropped for lack of variability). An overall Multivariate Analysis of Variance (MANOVA) with the 56 remaining items indicated statistically significant main effects for Group, $F(2, 225) = 15.5, p < .001$, and Item, $T(55, 171) = 52.8, p < .001$, and a statistically significant Group x Item interaction, $T(110, 340) = 4.05, p < .001$. [Hotelling's Trace (*T*) was used as a conservative estimate in all repeated measures analyses.] This was followed by separate Group x Item Analyses of Variance (ANOVAs).

Our conservative assumption was that Group and Child Age were the two primary independent variables that would be expected to be related to quality of life. Thus, items that clearly bore no relation to either of these variables—items that were not statistically significant ($p > .10$) on either the follow-up ANOVAs or LSDs, or that did not correlate with Child Age—were deleted from further analyses. As such, 12 more items were deleted, leaving 44 items in the QLQ.

Factor analysis. A maximum likelihood factor analysis with varimax rotation was conducted with the 44 remaining items. Analyses with 2 to 10 factors were explored with a liberal cut-off value of .30 being the initial minimum accepted loading for an item on a factor. When forcing two factors, many items did not load on either factor. Analyses forcing five or more factors produced short (three or fewer items) and potentially unreliable scales. A three-factor solution (Behavior Problem, Developmental Level, Satisfaction/Support) accounted for 28.2% of the variance. A four-factor solution, accounting for 32.3% of the variance, included these three factors plus a factor for Family Psychiatric History. Using this conceptually appealing four-factor solution, we sought to further reduce the length of the scales by deleting those items loading less than .40 on a factor (a more conservative cutoff value) or having item-total correlations (reliability analysis) less than .20; 16 additional items were deleted.

The final four-factor solution using the remaining 28 items, accounted for 44.5% of the variance, $X^2(297) = 710.2, p < .001$, and can be seen in Table 2. Subscale scores (simple sums) were calculated for each of the four factors, as well as a QLQ Total Score. For all subscales, higher scores indicate a greater quality of life (i.e., fewer behavior problems and developmental delays; fewer psychiatric problems in the family history; and greater satisfaction with interactions, activities, and assistance).

Test-retest reliability. A high degree of test-retest reliability was evident for three of the subscales and the total score: Developmental Level, $r(33) = .97, p < .001$; Family Psychiatric History, $r(33) = .97, p < .001$; Satisfaction/Support, $r(33) = .85, p < .001$; and QLQ Total Score, $r(33) = .94, p < .001$. There was an acceptable level of test-retest reliability for the Behavior Problem subscale, $r(33) = .66, p < .001$. Additionally, there were no statistically significant differences between the means for each subscale and the total score on the test and retest, respectively; Behavior Problem: 21.1 ($SD = 3.9$) vs. 17.8 ($SD = 7.0$), Developmental Level: 23.1 ($SD = 9.4$) vs. 22.8 ($SD = 6.8$), Family Psychiatric History: 10.2 ($SD = 2.7$) vs. 10.5 ($SD = 2.6$), Satisfaction/Support: 32.8 ($SD = 6.1$) vs. 31.8 ($SD = 6.3$), QLQ Total Score: 87.2 ($SD = 15.2$) vs. 82.8 ($SD = 18.7$).

Internal consistency. The results from an examination of internal consistency are provided in Table 3, showing excellent psychometric properties for all QLQ subscales and the final 28-item scale. Correlations among the four subscales were generally low, and ranged from .15 to .42 (mean = .28), with corrected subscale to total scale correlations ranging from .27 to .47, with a mean of .40 (Cronbach's *alpha* = .61). The correlations of each subscale with the QLQ Total Score were higher: Behavior Problem, $r(228) = .74$, $p < .001$; Developmental Level, $r(228) = .75$, $p < .001$; Family Psychiatric History, $r(228) = .43$, $p < .001$; and Satisfaction/Support, $r(228) = .75$, $p < .001$.

Group differences. Table 4 presents the group means for the QLQ subscales and total score. An overall MANOVA with the four subscales indicated a main effect for Group, $T(8, 442) = 15.9$, $p < .001$. Follow-up ANOVAs (and post hoc LSD tests, $p < .05$) showed statistically significant group differences on each subscale: Behavior Problem, $F(2, 225) = 13.3$, $p < .001$ (Group TD > Groups BP and DD); Developmental Level, $F(2, 225) = 49.1$, $p < .001$ (Groups TD and BP > Group DD); Family Psychiatric History, $F(2, 225) = 5.2$, $p < .01$ (Groups TD and BP > Group DD); and Satisfaction/Support, $F(2, 225) = 4.8$, $p < .01$ (Group TD > Groups BP and DD). In a separate ANOVA, the three groups differed from each other on the QLQ Total Score, $F(2, 225) = 27.2$, $p < .001$ (LSD: $p < .01$; Group TD > Group BP > Group DD).

QLQ and demographic variables. Mothers' age, child gender, and family income were not significantly related to any subscale scores or QLQ Total Score. Age of the child significantly negatively correlated with two of the subscales [Behavior Problem: $r(224) = -.36$, $p < .001$; Developmental Level: $r(224) = -.19$, $p < .01$] and the QLQ Total Score, $r(224) = -.28$, $p < .001$. Population was negatively correlated with all but one subscale [Behavior Problem: $r(228) = -.16$, $p < .05$; Developmental Level: $r(228) = -.17$, $p < .05$; Satisfaction/Support: $r(228) = -.15$, $p < .05$], and QLQ Total Score, $r(228) = -.21$, $p < .01$. Mother's educational level was positively correlated with Satisfaction/Support, $r(225) = .23$, $p < .001$, and QLQ Total Score, $r(225) = .14$, $p < .05$.

A MANOVA (4 Subscales x 2 Race/Ethnicity), $T(4, 222) = 4.9$, $p < .001$, showed Race/Ethnicity (Non-White as compared to White, respectively) to be related to higher scores on Family Psychiatric History, $F(1, 225) = 7.1$, $p < .01$ ($M = 10.9$, $SD = 1.7$ vs. $M = 10.0$, $SD = 2.6$), and lower scores on Satisfaction/Support, $F(1, 225) = 6.0$, $p < .05$ ($M = 32.8$, $SD = 5.5$ vs. $M = 34.9$, $SD = 6.2$); race/ethnicity was unrelated to QLQ Total Score. The differences on these subscales are small and are potentially related to demographic differences between Non-White and White mothers, respectively, including: younger age, $F(1, 223) = 15.3$, $p < .001$ ($M = 25.9$ years, $SD = 5.9$ vs. $M = 29.4$ years, $SD = 6.3$), lower annual income, $F(1, 163) = 21.4$, $p < .001$ ($M = \$24,490.49$, $SD = \$26,814.92$ vs. $M = \$59,784.37$, $SD = \$48,385.31$), and greater population, $F(1, 225) = 12.9$, $p < .001$ ($M = 306,419$, $SD = 257,721$ vs. $M = 165,277$, $SD = 301,812$). Further, Non-White mothers (19%) were less likely than White mothers (49%) to have a college degree, $X^2(5) = 20.9$, $p < .001$.

Table 2

Four-Factor Solution for QLQ

Item Number and Description / Factor	Behavior Problems	Developmental Level	Family Psychiatric History	Satisfaction/ Support
1. Bathing: Frequency of behavior problems	.71			
2. Bathing: Ease	.59			
3. Feeding: Frequency of behavior problems	.81			
4. Feeding: Ease	.70			
5. Dressing: Frequency of behavior problems	.70			
6. Dressing: Ease	.57			
7. Problem behavior used to communicate	.41			
8. Gross motor skills		.70		
9. Fine motor skills		.77		
10. Communication skills		.58		
11. Cognitive skills		.80		
12. Social-emotional skills		.70		
13. Adaptive skills		.63		
14. Play skills		.60		
15. Family history: Anxiety disorders			.81	
16. Family history: Mood disorders			.78	
17. Family history: ADHD			.45	
18. Regular bedtime routine				.42
19. Problems falling asleep				.43
20. Overall interactions with child				.42

Item Number and Description / Factor	Behavior Problems	Developmental Level	Family Psychiatric History	Satisfaction/ Support
21. Overall interactions with family				.68
22. Family activities at home				.64
23. Interactions with family at home				.64
24. Visits from relatives				.49
25. Help provided by family and friends				.54
26. Interactions with those providing help				.54
27. Overall quality of life: Child				.56
28. Overall quality of life: Parent (mother)				.60

Note. See Appendix A for full wording of questions.

Table 3

Measures of Internal Consistency for QLQ Subscales and Total Scale

Scale / Statistic	Number of Items	Inter-Item Correlations Mean (Range)	Corrected Item-Total Correlations Mean (Range)	Cronbach's *Alpha*
Behavior Problem	7	.24 (.21 - .75)	.60 (.41 - .75)	.85
Developmental Level	7	.51 (.38 - .69)	.66 (.61 - .74)	.87
Family Psychiatric History	3	.48 (.38 - .67)	.58 (.42 - .66)	.74
Satisfaction/Support	11	.31 (.13 - .66)	.49 (.36 - .57)	.82
QLQ Total Scale	28	.21 (-.10 - .75)	.43 (.16 - .58)	.88

Table 4

Group Means (Standard Deviations) for QLQ Subscales and Total Score

Scale (# of items)	Typical Development (n = 102)	Behavior Problem (n = 43)	Developmental Delay (n = 83)
Behavior Problem (7)	23.4 (4.2)[a]	20.2 (5.5)[b]	19.8 (5.7)[b]
Developmental Level (7)	26.4 (3.4)[a]	25.4 (2.8)[a]	19.8 (6.5)[b]
Family Psychiatric History (3)	10.7 (1.9)[a]	10.5 (2.2)[a]	9.6 (2.9)[b]
Satisfaction/Support (11)	35.6 (5.4)[a]	32.6 (5.7)[b]	33.6 (6.7)[b]
QLQ Total Score (28)	96.2 (9.7)[a]	88.8 (10.9)[b]	82.8 (15.5)[c]

Note. Possible ranges for scores are: Behavior Problem = 0 to 28; Developmental Level = 0 to 28; Family Psychiatric History = 0 to 12; Satisfaction/Support = 0 to 44; QLQ Total Score = 0 to 112.

[a, b, c] Within scales (rows), groups with different letters are significantly different from each other (see text), LSD, $p < .05$.

Discussion

As a key goal of early intervention programs is improvement of quality of life for the birth-to-three-year-old child and her/his family, it is self-evident that a psychometrically sound measure of quality of life would be useful to evaluate such improvements. We have presented the development and evaluation of a measure that may fulfill that need. The Quality of Life Questionnaire for Families of Young Children with Developmental Delays (QLQ-FYCDD) is a unique tool in several respects. First, it was developed for a specific population; that is, children three years or younger with developmental delays. We included in the instrument development and evaluation studies both children with problem behaviors and children without delays or behavior problems. The Phase II sample also represents mothers with diversity in race/ethnicity, income, education, and area of residence population size. The final version of the QLQ is short, taking less than 10 minutes to complete, and covers both child (i.e., behavior problems, developmental delays, quality of interactions) and family (e.g., family psychiatric history, quality of child/parent and general family interactions, help and support) issues. It is thus more likely to be completed by busy mothers with a young child with a developmental delay, and it is focused on those issues that the literature (Morrow et al., 2010; Raat et al., 2007; Robitail et al., 2007) and our measure development process show to be most relevant. Finally, the measure was shown to have good test-retest reliability and excellent internal consistency (i.e., high consistency within subscales; low overlap among scales).

The four subscales showed group differences consistent with the goals of the measure. The groups representing children with behavior problems and developmental delays had lower scores on both the Behavior Problem and Satisfaction/Support subscales, indicating more problems and less satisfaction and support than for the children without problems or delays. Further, the group of children with developmental delays scored lower on Developmental Level, thus differentiating it from the other two groups. Lastly, all three groups of children differed on the QLQ Total Score, with the mothers of the children with developmental delays reporting the lowest quality of life. Thus, this measure performs in a manner consistent with the expected differences among the groups.

Of further importance are the relations found between scores on the QLQ and various demographic variables. Correlational analyses showed that the "older" children within this sample of children under age 36 months were more likely to exhibit behavior problems and developmental delays, and, thus, lower quality of life. This makes sense as delays and problems become more and more evident as children grow older yet fall further behind developmentally. Of interest, the relation between QLQ scores and population of the city of residence suggests lower quality of life for those living in more densely populated areas. Alternately, this relation may suggest that families of children with more problems and delays move to areas likely to have more services. Finally, we note the racial/ethnic differences in several QLQ subscale scores, notably Satisfaction/Support. The initial evidence presented here suggests that this tentative relation is not itself clinically meaningful, but is more likely explained by variables related to race/ethnicity (e.g., age of mother, income, education) rather than racial/ethnic differences (i.e., Non-White as compared to White), per se.

Limitations

Along with the methodological improvements over prior studies (e.g., detailed report of item development and reduction, establishment of psychometric properties including test-retest reliability, greater ethnic diversity in the sample), some limitations are evident. A larger sample of professionals and variety of care-givers (e.g., fathers and agency staff, in addition to mothers) might have been used in Phase I for face and content validation. Further, in Phase II, both a greater variety of care-givers and a greater geographic distribution (beyond four southern states) would improve generalizability. The test-retest sample was not a random sample of the participants; those "volunteering" for the retest may have been a biased sample. Finally, a stricter requirement for factor loadings (i.e., higher than .40) would reduce the number of items on the QLQ; although this could then come at the expense of reliability, construct validity, and generalizability (Shadish, Cook, & Campbell, 2002).

Future Directions

Several future studies immediately present themselves, including an expanded range of care-givers, and geographic and racial/ethnic diversity. With the increasing number of Hispanics and Asian-Americans in the U.S. population (both of which are under-represented in this study), data will need to be gathered on a wider range of racial/ethnic groups, along with increased exploration of the variables that may be associated with racial/ethnic differences in QLQ scores. As the United States becomes increasingly multi-lingual, the primary language of the respondents will also need to be considered. The questions that are raised by the relations between QLQ scores and population of the area of residence can also be addressed through evaluation of service availability and patterns of residence (e.g., Did a family move to a particular area prior to or after recognizing a need for services? Was a move related to service availability in a particular area?). It will also be important to compare results on the QLQ to other measures of psychological health, impact of care, satisfaction with services, measures of social support and social networks, and formal measures of adaptive behavior and developmental delay. Such analyses will evaluate the concurrent and construct validity of the QLQ, along with providing needed information on additional factors contributing to quality of life.

A critical direction is to establish the clinical significance of scores on the QLQ subscales and the QLQ Total Score. Out of a possible Total Score of 112, the "typically" developing group had a mean score representing 86% of the possible range (mean of 96/maximum of 112); the behavior problem and development delay groups were at 79% and 74%, respectively. If using the QLQ as a repeated measure of quality of life in a service setting, it remains to be seen what aspects of services to children and families will impact QLQ scores and how much of a change in scores reflects actual clinical improvement (or decline). Our test-retest data suggest a five-point variation in QLQ Total Score over one week; this difference is likely to represent measure variability and not actual change.

In closing, the Quality of Life Questionnaire for Families of Young Children with Developmental Delays is presented as a psychometrically sound instrument for the assessment of quality of life in families with young children with developmental delays. The initial findings suggest that it can capture quality of life differences between families and children with developmental delays and those with behavior problems or who are typically developing. It can be used to direct attention to broad quality of life issues that affect the families of these children, and thus point toward areas for intervention and service delivery. Further research will illuminate whether it can also be used to evaluate the impact of those services.

References

Brotherson, M. J., Oakland, M. J., Secrist-Mertz, C., Litchfield, R., & Larson, K. (1995). Quality of life issues for families who make the decision to use a feeding tube for their child with disabilities. *Journal of the Association for Persons with Severe Handicaps, 20,* 202-212.

Brown, W., & Brown, C. (1993). Defining eligibility for early intervention. In W. Brown, S. K. Thurman, & L. F. Pearl (Eds.), *Family-centered early intervention with infants and toddlers* (pp. 21-42). Baltimore: Paul H. Brookes.

Cummins, R. A., McCabe, M. P., Romeo, Y., & Gullone, E. (1994). The comprehensive quality of life scale (ComQol): Instrument development and psychometric evaluation on college staff and students. *Educational and Psychological Measurement, 54,* 372-382.

French, D. J., Christie, M. J., & Sowden, A. J. (1994). The reproducibility of the Childhood Asthma Questionnaires: Measures of quality of life for children with asthma aged 4-16 years. *Quality of Life Research, 3,* 215-224.

Green, C. W., Gardner, S. M., & Reid, D. H. (1997). Increasing indices of happiness among people with profound multiple disabilities: A program replication and component analysis. *Journal of Applied Behavior Analysis, 30,* 217-227.

Hall, T., Horner-Johnson, W., Krahn, G. L., & Lamb, G. (2011). Examining functional content in widely used health-related quality of life scales. *Rehabilitation Psychology, 56,* 94-99.

Leibowitz, J. M., McCalin, J. W., Evans, E. A., Ruma, P., & Rauner, T. (1994). Client perceptions of quality of life in accredited and nonaccredited community residential facilities. *Journal of Developmental and Physical Disabilities, 6,* 339-346.

Moos, R. H., & Moos, B. (1981). *Revised Family Environment Scale.* Palo Alto, CA: Consulting Psychologists.

Morrow, A. M., Quine, S., Heaton, M. D., & Craig, J. C. (2010). Assessing quality of life in paediatric clinical practice. *Journal of Paediatrics and Child Health, 46,* 323-328.

Nathan, P. C., Furlong, W., Horsman, J., van Schaik, C., Rolland, M., Weitzman, S.,… Barr, R. D. (2004). Inter-observer agreement of a comprehensive health status classification system for preschool children among patients with Wilms' tumor or advanced neuroblastoma. *Quality of Life Research, 13,* 1707-1714.

Nunnally, J. C., & Bernstein, I. H. (1994). *Psychometric theory* (3rd ed.). New York: McGraw-Hill.

Patrick, D. L., & Deyo, R. A. (1989). Generic and disease-specific measures in assessing health status and quality of life. *Medical Care, 27,* 217-232.

Pedlar, A., Lord, J., & Van Loon, M. (1990). Quality of life outcomes of supported employment. *Canadian Journal of Community Mental Health, 9,* 79-96.

Punpanich, W., Hays, R. D., Detels, R., Chokephaibulkit, K., Chantbuddhiwet, U., Leowsrisok, P., & Prasitsuebsal, W. (2010). Development of a culturally appropriate health-related quality of life measure for human immunodeficiency virus-infected children in Thailand. *Journal of Paediatrics and Child Health, 47*, 27-33.

Raat, H., Landgraf, J. M., Oostenbrink, R., Moll, H. A., & Essink-Bot, M. L. (2007). Reliability and validity of the Infant and Toddler Quality of Life Questionnaire (ITQOL) in a general population and respiratory disease sample. *Quality of Life Research, 16*, 445-460.

Robitail, S., Ravens-Sieberer, U., Simeoni, M. C., Rajmil, L., Bruil, J., Power, M.,... Auquier, P. (2007). Testing the structural and cross-cultural validity of the KIDSCREEN-27 quality of life questionnaire. *Quality of Life Research, 16*, 1335-1345.

Russell, K. M., Hudson, M., Long, A., & Phipps, S. (2006). Assessment of health-related quality of life in children with cancer: Consistency and agreement between parent and child reports. *Cancer, 106*, 2267-2274.

Schalock, R. L. (1994). Quality of life, quality enhancement, and quality assurance: Implications for program planning and evaluation in the field of mental retardation and developmental disabilities. *Evaluation and Program Planning, 17*, 121-131.

Schalock, R. L., Brown, I., Brown, R., Cummins, R. A., Felce, D., Matikka, L.,... Parmenter, T. (2002). Conceptualization, measurement, and application of quality of life for persons with intellectual disabilities: Report of an international panel of experts. *Mental Retardation. 40*, 457-470.

Shadish, W. R., Cook, T. D., & Campbell, D. T. (2002). *Experimental and quasi-experimental designs for generalized causal inference.* New York: Houghton Mifflin.

Spieth, L. E., & Harris, C. V. (1996). Assessment of health-related quality of life in children and adolescents: An integrative review. *Journal of Pediatric Psychology, 21*, 175-193.

Wang, M., Summers, J. A., Little, T., Turnbull, A., Poston, D., & Mannan, H. (2006). Perspectives of fathers and mothers of children in early intervention programmes in assessing family quality of life. *Journal of Intellectual Disability Research, 50*, 977-988.

Yoo, H. J., Ra, Y. S., Park, H. J., Lai, J. S., Cella, D., Shin, H. Y., & Kim, D. S. (2010). Agreement between pediatric brain tumor patients and parent proxy reports regarding the Pediatric Functional Assessment of Cancer Therapy-Childhood Brain Tumor Survivors Questionnaire, Version 2. *Cancer, 116*, 3674-3682.

Young, B., Rice, H., Dixon-Woods, M., Colver, A. F., & Parkinson, K. N. (2007). A qualitative study of the health-related quality of life of disabled children. *Developmental Medicine and Child Neurology, 49*, 660-665.

Author Note

The first author completed this paper as her dissertation at West Virginia University. We acknowledge and thank the Psychology Department Alumni Committee and the Eberly College of Arts and Sciences for financial support of the project.

Appendix A
Quality of Life Questionnaire for
Families of Young Children with Developmental Delays

1. How often does your child have behavior problems during bathing activities?
   Always   Often   Sometimes   Rarely   Never

2. How easy or hard is it for you to complete bathing activities with your child?
   Very Hard   Hard   Neutral/Unsure   Easy   Very Easy

3. How often does your child have behavior problems during feeding activities?
   Always   Often   Sometimes   Rarely   Never

4. How easy or hard is it for you to complete feeding activities with your child?
   Very Hard   Hard   Neutral/Unsure   Easy   Very Easy

5. How often does your child have behavior problems during dressing activities?
   Always   Often   Sometimes   Rarely   Never

6. How easy or hard is it for you to complete dressing activities with your child?
   Very Hard   Hard   Neutral/Unsure   Easy   Very Easy

7. How often does your child use problem behavior to tell you that he/she does not want something (e.g., tantrums, self-injurious behavior, aggression)?
   Always   Often   Sometimes   Rarely   Never

8. How much of a problem does your child have with gross motor skills (e.g., sitting, walking)?
   Severe   Moderate   Mild   Somewhat   Not at All

9. How much of a problem does your child have with fine motor skills (e.g., putting pegs in a pegboard, grasping small objects)?
   Severe   Moderate   Mild   Somewhat   Not at All

10. How much of a problem does your child have with communication skills (e.g., babbling, talking)?

      Severe   Moderate   Mild   Somewhat   Not at All

11. How much of a problem does your child have with cognitive skills (e.g., child turns to look at sound, child correctly activates a simple toy)?

      Severe   Moderate   Mild   Somewhat   Not at All

12. How much of a problem does your child have with social/emotional skills (e.g., displays affection toward caregiver, responds to routines)?

      Severe   Moderate   Mild   Somewhat   Not at All

13. How much of a problem does your child have with adaptive skills (e.g., eating, toilet training, dressing)?

      Severe   Moderate   Mild   Somewhat   Not at All

14. How much of a problem does your child have with play skills (e.g., takes turns, plays independently)?

      Severe   Moderate   Mild   Somewhat   Not at All

15. Rate how much of a problem anxiety disorders are in your family history (e.g., your immediate family and those relatives who live in your home).

      Severe   Moderate   Mild   Somewhat   Not at All

16. Rate how much of a problem depression and mood disorders are in your family history (e.g., your immediate family and those relatives who live in your home).

      Severe   Moderate   Mild   Somewhat   Not at All

17. Rate how much of a problem attention deficit hyperactivity disorder (ADHD) is in your family history (e.g., your immediate family and those relatives who live in your home).

      Severe   Moderate   Mild   Somewhat   Not at All

18. Does your child have a bedtime routine?

      Never   Rarely   Sometimes   Often   Always

19. Rate how often your child has problems falling asleep.

      Always   Often   Sometimes   Rarely   Never

20. How would you rate the overall quality of your interactions with your child?
Very Negative   Negative   Neutral/Unsure   Positive   Very Positive

21. How satisfied are you with interactions you have with family members who live with you?
Not at All Satisfied   Dissatisfied   Neutral/Unsure   Satisfied   Very Satisfied

22. How satisfied are you with the types of activities that your family does together at home?
Not at All Satisfied   Dissatisfied   Neutral/Unsure   Satisfied   Very Satisfied

23. How satisfied are you with your family's interactions in the home (e.g., eating meals, watching TV, playing games)?
Not at All Satisfied   Dissatisfied   Neutral/Unsure   Satisfied   Very Satisfied

24. How satisfied are you with the frequency of visits you receive from relatives?
Not at All Satisfied   Dissatisfied   Neutral/Unsure   Satisfied   Very Satisfied

25. Families often have other relatives or friends to whom they turn for help. How satisfied are you with the help they give you when they do help you?
Not at All Satisfied   Dissatisfied   Neutral/Unsure   Satisfied   Very Satisfied

26. How satisfied are you with the quality of the interactions that you have with those relatives and friends who do help your family?
Not at All Satisfied   Dissatisfied   Neutral/Unsure   Satisfied   Very Satisfied

27. How would you rate the overall quality of life (e.g., how much your family and your child enjoy different possibilities and experiences, such as social relationships, living conditions, health) for your child?
Very Negative   Negative   Neutral/Unsure   Positive   Very Positive

28. How would you rate your overall quality of life (e.g., how much your family and your child enjoy different possibilities and experiences, such as social relationships, living conditions, health) as a parent?
Very Negative   Negative   Neutral/Unsure   Positive   Very Positive

Interrater Reliability of the Classroom Assessment Scoring System – Pre-K (CLASS Pre-K)

Lia E. Sandilos & James C. DiPerna
Pennsylvania State University

The purpose of the current study was to evaluate the reliability of scores from the Classroom Assessment Scoring System – Pre-kindergarten Version (CLASS Pre-K; Pianta, La Paro, & Hamre, 2008). Ten raters completed a total of 32 observations across 12 preschool classrooms. Interrater reliability estimates of the scores were calculated using percent-within-one (PWO) analysis, percentage of exact agreement, intraclass correlations, weighted kappa, and Cohen's kappa. Results of this study indicated that interrater agreement using the PWO criterion was comparable to the interrater agreement reported in the CLASS technical manual and previous research. The more stringent indices, however, were lower than those reported in previous studies of the CLASS Pre-K.

The quality of children's relationships with their primary teachers has been identified as one of the most powerful factors related to student learning and future academic success (La Paro & Pianta, 2000; Pianta, La Paro, Payne, Cox, & Bradley, 2002). The theoretical basis for high quality education suggests that interactions between students and adults are the primary mechanism for facilitating student learning and development (Pianta, La Paro, & Hamre, 2008; Rutter & Maughan, 2002). Didactic theory also places importance on the way in which educators utilize the materials with which they are provided in order to engage children in active learning (Rutter & Maughan).

Two theoretical models, the Bioecological model (Bronfenbrenner & Morris, 1998) and General Systems Theory (Pianta, 1999), provide useful frameworks for understanding child development in relation to the classroom environment. In the Bioecological model, development is viewed as a process that occurs not only within the child, but also via interaction within the child's environment. Therefore, interventions that impact social processes with teachers, peers, and schools will, in turn, influence the child's growth (Rimm-Kaufman & Chiu, 2007). General Systems Theory, a framework regarding the complex relationships between biological, ecological, social and other living systems, can also be applied to experiences within the classroom setting (Pianta). In this theory, teachers' relationships are critical to children's development, and these relationships are vehicles by which

Correspondence concerning this article should be addressed to Lia Sandilos, School Psychology, The Pennsylvania State University, 125 CEDAR Building University Park, PA 16802. E-mail: les207@psu.edu.

children's needs can be addressed. Teachers serve as role models and regulate behavior through interactions, relationships, and behavior management strategies. As a result, children's strengths and needs are not just defined by their academic abilities; rather they also are seen as the result of the educator's teaching methods in the classroom setting (Rimm-Kaufman & Chiu).

Exemplary early education programs provide support for social and emotional functioning, use consistent behavior management methods, establish positive student-teacher relationships, and utilize language modeling (Howes et al., 2008; Pianta, 1999). According to Hamre and Pianta (2005), teacher warmth and support help children's achievement and adjustment. To pinpoint these factors, researchers need to collect relevant information about classroom processes and related outcomes (Pianta et al., 2008), and one method for collecting information on the classroom environment is systematic direct observation.

Early Childhood Classroom Observation Systems

The utilization of direct observation in classrooms has helped to elucidate the nature of effective teaching (Good & Brophy, 2000). Although the first observation scales date to the 1940s, Sandefur and Bressler (1970) identified the 1960s as a time when the majority of early systems were developed. In their seminal review, Sandefur and Bressler grouped observation systems into affective systems (concerned with the emotional climate of the classroom), cognitive systems (concerned with intellectual activities which improve cognitive processes and skills), and multidimensional systems (assessed both the affective and cognitive domains). Many of the scales emphasized analysis of interactions between student and teacher.

Since Sandefur and Bressler's (1970) review, observation systems have continued to directly measure effective teaching strategies that promote positive academic, social, and emotional growth in children. In a recent review of early childhood classroom observation measures and environmental rating scales, Grinder (2007) identified several scales for the early education environment, such as Early Childhood Environment Rating Scale- Revised (ECERS-R; Harms, Clifford, & Cryer, 1998), Early Language and Literacy Classroom Observation (ELLCO; Smith & Dickinson, 2002; Smith, Brady, & Clark-Chiarelli, 2008) and CLASS Pre-K (Pianta et al., 2008).

The ECERS-R assesses multiple characteristics of preschool, kindergarten, and child-care programs. This measure examines seven distinct components of the classroom: Space and Furnishings, Personal Care Routines, Language-Reasoning, Activities, Interaction, Program Structure, and Parents and Staff. These subscales evaluate a wide-range of factors that include, but are not limited to, the following: amount of indoor space available, presence of furniture for both play and relaxation, number of meals or snacks provided, employment of safety and health practices, availability of books, and quality of staff-child interactions. The ECERS-R also specifically addresses issues surrounding children with disabilities and is intended to be sensitive to cultural differences (Harms et al., 1998).

Despite its widespread use, few studies have been published concerning the psychometric properties of scores from the ECERS-R (Perlman, Zellman, & Vi-Nhuan, 2004). Factor analytic findings regarding the structural validity of the ECERS-R indicated that the scale assesses one overall construct of classroom quality, as opposed to the seven distinct domains of classroom quality suggested by the authors (Perlman et al., 2004). Douglas (2004) noted that another limitation of the ECERS-R is that the scale does not capture the quality of teacher-child and peer interactions in the classroom, which has been shown to be an important component of early childhood education.

A second popular early childhood observation system is the ELLCO Pre-K. The ELLCO Pre-K observation tool has a narrower focus than the ECERS-R. It is designed to specifically assess the quality of language and literacy experiences in pre-kindergarten classroom settings (Smith & Dickinson, 2002). The ELLCO Pre-K classroom observation tool measures five key components of early literacy. The first two components (i.e., Classroom Structure and Curriculum) evaluate such factors as classroom content, organization, and management. The other three components (i.e., Language Environment, Books and Reading, and Print and Writing) include items that evaluate instructional efforts to build students' vocabulary, reading fluency, and reading comprehension (Smith et al., 2008). In addition to examining the instructional opportunities presented to students for language and literacy development, the ELLCO allows observers to assess the availability and quality of the literacy-related materials in the environment (i.e., books, writing products). However, the ELLCO is limited in that its primary use is to evaluate language and literacy, and the scale is not intended to be used as a comprehensive assessment of overall teaching quality on a typical school day.

In response to some of the limitations of previous early childhood observation systems, the CLASS Pre-K was developed to assess the quality of the pre-kindergarten classroom environment. The CLASS Pre-K is a relatively new system and the primary focus of the current study.[1] The goal of CLASS Pre-K is to examine the relationship between teachers and their students, as well as to assess the didactic techniques that teachers use in their classrooms (La Paro, Pianta, & Stuhlman, 2004). Three major domains of the classroom environment are assessed: Emotional Support, Classroom Organization, and Instructional Support. These domains are further divided into 10 dimensions. Emotional Support consists of Positive Climate, Negative Climate, Teacher Sensitivity, and Regard for Student Perspectives. Classroom Organization consists of Behavior Management, Productivity, and Instructional Learning Formats. Finally, Instructional Support is comprised of Concept Development, Quality of Feedback, and Language Modeling.

---

[1] Additional forms of the CLASS are now available at the elementary and secondary levels.

The CLASS Pre-K observation scale can be differentiated from the two afore-mentioned scales in that it incorporates a diverse set of characteristics that form unique constructs. These constructs focus on teacher-child interactions, evaluate didactic and behavior management techniques utilized by the teacher, and examine a teacher's use and implementation of the instructional materials in the classroom. Because the materials available in early education programs can vary widely, CLASS Pre-K is distinctive in that it assesses what teachers do with what they have, and it does not evaluate the quantity or quality of the materials accessible in the physical environment. Additionally, CLASS Pre-K is not restricted to one subject (e.g., reading instruction) and can be used during both structured and unstructured periods of the school day. Another difference between CLASS Pre-K and the aforementioned scales is that it does not contain a disabilities/cultural diversity component in the scale.

The CLASS Pre-K observation system was designed to provide a research-based framework to assess teaching quality in early childhood and elementary classrooms. Since the scale was first published in 2008, CLASS Pre-K has been widely adopted for use in research and evaluation in over 3,000 early childhood classrooms (Hamre, Goffin, & Kraft-Sayre, 2009). In addition, the CLASS Pre-K is one of the few observation scales that were piloted to assess the quality of Head Start classrooms nationwide (U.S. Department of Health and Human Services, 2008).

Educational researchers have assessed the relationship between CLASS Pre-K scores and a variety of academic and behavioral outcomes. These outcome variables include self-regulatory and adaptive behaviors, aggression, and progress in literacy (Buyse, Verschueren, & Doumen, 2011; Hamre et al., 2010; Pakarinen et al., 2010; Rimm-Kaufman, Curby, Grimm, Nathanson, & Brock, 2009). CLASS scores also have been used to analyze stability and change in dimensions of teaching quality over the course of one school day, as well as throughout the academic year (Curby, Rimm-Kaufman, & Ponitz, 2009; Malmberg, Hagger, Burn, Mutton, & Colls, 2010).

The authors of CLASS Pre-K report adequate interrater reliability of scores on CLASS Pre-K dimensions (.78 - .96). Average correlations between observation cycles[2] range from .68 to .88. Internal consistency coefficients for Cycles 2, 3, and 4 for preschool and third grade classrooms range from .76 to .90. Criterion-related validity estimates examining the relationship between CLASS Pre-K and ECERS-R range from .45 to .63 for "interaction" factors (extent to which classrooms promote teacher-child interactions, facilitate effective discipline, and encourage children to communicate) and .33 to .36 for "provision" factors (availability of materials). The low correlations between "provision" factors on the CLASS Pre-K and ECERS-R could be attributed to difference in the way each scale assesses materials. The ECERS-R evaluates "provision" factors by assessing the cleanliness of furnishings, the abundance of books accessible in the classroom, and the types of toys and

---

[2]   A CLASS cycle consists of 20 minutes of observation and 10 minutes of coding.

gross motor equipment available to the children (Harms et al., 1998). In contrast, CLASS Pre-K assesses "provision" factors solely based on how the teacher utilizes materials in the classroom to facilitate learning (Hamre, Mashburn, Pianta, & Locasle-Crouch, 2008; Pianta et al., 2008).

Need for Further Psychometric Evidence for CLASS Pre-K

Because observation systems are used to evaluate the quality of educational settings, educational researchers have placed emphasis on the development of standardized classroom observation measures with sufficient score validity and reliability. One of the challenges in developing and utilizing classroom observation instruments is finding ways of establishing score reliability between raters, or interrater reliability (Olswang, Svensson, Coggins, Beilinson, & Donaldson, 2006). Observation systems are particularly susceptible to error given the level of subjectivity involved in the assessment. To assess the interrater reliability of the scores on an observation system, two or more raters must observe the same event. If these raters produce parallel results (i.e., consistent scores across raters), then interrater reliability is evident (Suen, 1988).

Data reported in previous interrater reliability studies for CLASS Pre-K have been collected within the context of the structured professional development workshops. As part of the CLASS Pre-K training program, trainees watch multiple videotaped classroom sessions and practice coding their observations. At the end of the training, the potential CLASS Pre-K users take a reliability test in which they watch and code videotaped classroom segments. Interrater reliability of scores is computed between the ratings of trained or "master" coders and the newly trained users. Although this technique has yielded high interrater reliability estimates (approximately .87), the data were collected via videotaped observations in a controlled environment (Hamre et al., 2008; Pianta et al., 2008).

In a 2004 study, La Paro et al. trained 20 individuals to use CLASS Pre-K. These trainees had four opportunities to achieve the CLASS Pre-K "certification" standard[3] for interrater reliability ($\geq$ 80% agreement) by observing videos of preschool classrooms. Eighteen of the trainees achieved this certification standard. No further interrater agreement estimates, however, were reported from real-time observations completed within preschool classrooms.

Howes et al. (2008) also examined interrater reliability through the CLASS Pre-K training and certification process. Two separate trainings were held to certify observers for data collection. Using data collected during both trainings, weighted

---

[3]   The CLASS Pre-K reliability certification process occurs at the conclusion of a formal two-day training. The trainees score five 20-minute videotaped segments from classrooms, and their scores are compared with those of the master coders. Trainees who pass with a PWO of 80% or higher are certified in CLASS Pre-K (Teachstone Training LLC, 2011). Practitioners interested in using CLASS Pre-K should visit the following website for training and certification information: http://www.teachstone.org

kappa coefficients were calculated for each of the 10 dimensions across all of the trainees' ratings. The *kappa* coefficients were reported to have a mean of approximately .65 for each dimension in both trainings. As with the La Paro et al. (2004) study, the interrater agreement indices reported in the Howes et al. study were based on data collected by certified observers. No interrater reliability data were reported from actual classroom observations beyond the training sessions.

Because CLASS Pre-K is a new, complex system with multiple levels and dimensions, it may be vulnerable to error across raters, particularly during real-time observations. The purpose of the current study was to evaluate the interrater reliability of scores on the CLASS Pre-K for pre-kindergarten classrooms. The primary hypothesis was that dimension and domain scores of the CLASS Pre-K demonstrate acceptable interrater reliability for real-time observations in a pre-kindergarten setting.

Method

Participants

Teachers and children from 12 pre-kindergarten classrooms across four private full-day preschools participated in this study. All of the lead teachers in the participating classrooms were female. Eleven (91%) of the teachers were Caucasian and one (9%) was African American. Approximately 20 children were enrolled in each participating class (49.2% female, 50.8% male) and 84% of the participating children were Caucasian. The remaining children were Asian or African American.

Measures

CLASS Pre-K. The purpose of CLASS Pre-K is to examine the quality of the teacher-student relationships, as well as to assess the way in which teachers utilize the material with which they are provided (La Paro et al., 2004; Pianta et al., 2008). Raters can observe a classroom for one to four cycles. CLASS Pre-K yields individual scores for each of the 10 dimensions (Positive Climate, Negative Climate, Teacher Sensitivity, Regard for Student Perspectives, Behavior Management, Productivity, Instructional Learning Formats, Concept Development, Quality of Feedback, and Language Modeling) within each cycle, as well as a score for each dimension that is averaged across the number of completed observation cycles. Each dimension is rated on a 7-point scale ranging from *Low* (1-2) to *Middle* (3-5) to *High* (6-7). To assist observers in differentiating between scale ranges on each dimension (e.g., Low Positive Climate vs. Middle Positive Climate), the manual provides detailed examples and anecdotes reflecting what raters are likely to observe in a classroom environment falling in that range. Finally, the three domain scores (Emotional Support, Classroom Organization, Instructional Support) are calculated

Table 1

Definitions and Examples of CLASS Pre-K Domains and Dimensions

Domain/Dimension	Definition	Examples of Observed Classroom Practices
Emotional Support	Support for social-emotional functioning in classroom	
Positive Climate	Level of positive teacher-student, peer-peer interaction	Using positive verbal statements (e.g., great job!)
Negative Climate	Level of teacher-student, peer-peer negativity	Raising voice, rolling eyes
Teacher Sensitivity	Awareness/responsiveness to academic/emotional needs	Expressing concern for well-being; reflecting emotions
Regard for Student Perspectives	Emphasis on student interests/autonomy	Providing opportunity for autonomy (e.g., class helper)
Classroom Management	Behavior management and classroom organization	
Behavior Management	Capacity to manage student behavior	Using behavioral techniques (e.g., positive reinforcement)
Productivity	Management of time during school day	Consistent provision of activities; rapid transitions
Instructional Learning Formats	Degree of student interest and learning	Using diverse materials; student engagement
Instructional Support	Promoting language skills and cognitive development	
Concept Development	Techniques used to promote analytical thinking skills	Linking material to students' lives
Quality of Feedback	Use of feedback to strengthen skill development	Scaffolding new skills
Language Modeling	Techniques used to increase language development	Using and defining new vocabulary

Note. Definitions and examples were based on the CLASS Pre-K manual (Pianta et al., 2008).

by summing the average dimension scores that fall into each domain and dividing by the number of dimensions in that domain. See Table 1 for brief descriptions of CLASS dimensions and domains.

As noted earlier, the authors of CLASS Pre-K report adequate interrater agreement (.78 - .96.) and internal consistency reliabilities (.76 - .90). Criterion-related validity estimates examining the relationship between CLASS Pre-K and ECERS-R have varied from .33 to .63 (Hamre et al., 2008; Pianta et al., 2008). However, research is needed regarding interrater reliability of CLASS Pre-K scores when observations are completed in real-time within the classroom environment. Examining interrater reliability of CLASS Pre-K observations collected under such conditions was the primary goal of the current study.

Procedure

Prior to recruiting teachers, the directors of each preschool were informed of the study through a scripted phone call. Once verbal consent was received from the preschool directors, a written letter describing both the purpose and the process of the observations was sent to each pre-kindergarten teacher. The written letter included consent forms, which were to be sent back to the principal investigator. Additionally, approximately 350 letters were sent home to the parents of the children in 17 pre-kindergarten classrooms explaining, in detail, the nature of the study. Parents were given the opportunity to have their child excluded from the observation process. If a parent chose this option, no observations of that child's pre-kindergarten class were conducted. Ultimately, 3 parents and 2 teachers opted out of the study, bringing the number of participating classrooms to 12.

Ten graduate students (9 females, 1 male) served as observers in the study. Each of these students had previously completed formal coursework in educational observation and assessment prior to their involvement in the current study. The principal researcher was a doctoral-level school psychology graduate student who was formally trained in CLASS Pre-K. Additional observers then were trained in use of the CLASS Pre-K by the principal researcher. To meet certification requirements, all observers had to view and code a videotaped clip of a pre-kindergarten classroom. The trainees' scores were compared to those of the principal researcher, and all trainees had to meet the accuracy standard identified by the authors of the CLASS-Pre-K (PWO $\geq$ .80; Pianta et al., 2008) before conducting observations for the current study.

Observers traveled together to observe in the designated classroom sites approximately four times per week for 8 weeks. A total of 32 observations were conducted over a 2-month period. All raters used the CLASS Pre-K observation scale to assess the pre-kindergarten classroom environment. Nineteen pairs of raters, comprised of different combinations of the 10 data collectors, observed together once, while 6 pairs observed together more than once. However, the same pair of data collectors never observed in the same classroom on multiple occasions. While conducting the observations, data collectors sat several feet away from each other. The observers also were instructed to not share ratings after conducting their observations. One CLASS Pre-K cycle consists of 20 minutes of observation and 10 minutes of coding. The maximum set of four cycles used in CLASS Pre-K was shortened to two cycles in order to allow for multiple observations to be completed in a day.[4] Thus, raters observed for two 30-minute cycles, totaling 1 hour. At the end of each observation cycle, both observers separately scored all categories in the CLASS Pre-K scoring system

Data Analyses

The primary interrater reliability index reported in both the CLASS Pre-K technical manual and previously published research is the percent-within-one (PWO) analysis (Hamre et al., 2008; Pianta et al., 2008, La Paro et al., 2004). Because PWO was the primary indicator of interrater reliability reported in the CLASS Pre-K manual, PWO was considered as one of the reliability indices in this study as well. When calculating PWO, scores are considered to be in agreement if they fall within +/- 1 point of each other. Thus, for two raters to achieve 80% reliability on a CLASS Pre-K cycle, 8 out of 10 scores must fall within one point of each other. Because PWO is a fairly broad indicator of interrater agreement, additional, more conservative, interrater agreement estimates were calculated. These analyses included intraclass correlations, exact agreement, linearly weighted *kappa* and Cohen's (simple) *kappa*.

Intraclass correlations were calculated to determine the strength of the relationship of ratings between two observers on a single dimension (Fleiss & Cohen, 1973; Shrout & Fleiss, 1979). Because intraclass correlations provide an estimate of the relationship between two variables of the same unit or construct, the index is commonly used as a measure of interrater reliability (Field, 2009). Percentage of exact agreement was calculated to provide information regarding the precise agreement between raters. One limitation of percent-agreement indices is that the total percentage of agreement could be inflated if raters achieve similar scores by guessing or random chance (Wood, 2007). Thus, Cohen's *kappa* and weighted *kappa* also were calculated, as they are statistical indices in which chance agreement is taken into account in the agreement estimate (Cohen, 1960, 1968; Fleiss & Cohen, 1973).

Conceptually, Cohen's *kappa* is a more conservative estimate of reliability because it is the proportion of agreement between two raters after adjusting for the expected percentage of agreement that may occur through random chance (Cohen,

---

[4]   Data reported in the CLASS Pre-K manual indicate that dimension and domain scores for Cycle 1 and Cycle 2 correlate highly (.89 - .95) with Cycles 1 through 4 (Pianta et al., 2008).

1960; Wood, 2007). However, educational researchers have questioned whether Cohen's *kappa* may be an underestimate of reliability (Gwet, 2002; Nelson, Edwards, Gamishev, & Kozarev, 2007). Consequently, weighted *kappa* also was used as an index of interrater reliability in this study. Weighted *kappa* is a modification to Cohen's *kappa*, through which scores that are closer together (e.g., within 1 point) are given more weight than scores that are further apart.

In an effort to identify interpretive criteria for the indices used in this study, several sources were considered. There was some convergence between sources regarding the interpretation of reliability coefficients. As mentioned previously, the authors of CLASS Pre-K (Pianta et al., 2008) used a criterion of .80 for acceptable interrater reliability estimates based on a PWO analysis. In an earlier study of the CLASS, minimum criterion for weighted *kappa* was set at .60 (La Paro et al., 2004). Nunally and Bernstein (1994) suggested that a reliability coefficient of .70 is sufficient for a newly developed measure, but that research generally should require scores to demonstrate reliability coefficients of .80 or higher. Sattler (2001) recommended that reliability coefficients of .80 or higher be used for clinical and psycho-educational decision-making. Sattler also proposed that coefficients between .70 and .79 should be considered relatively reliable, coefficients between .60 and .69 should be considered marginally reliable, and those below .60 should be regarded as unreliable. Salvia and Ysseldyke (2007) suggested that standards of reliability for group data in an applied setting should be set at a minimum reliability of .60. These researchers also endorsed .80 as acceptable reliability criterion for low stakes decision-making.

Ultimately, ranges that converged across multiple sources were used to create the criteria for interpreting reliability data in this study. These criteria were as follows: < .60 = unacceptable, .60 to .69 = marginally acceptable, .70 to .79 = relatively acceptable, and ≥ .80 = acceptable. The criteria do not differentiate between different types of reliability indices, but they do reflect the reliability criteria that have been most commonly recommended in previous literature.

Results

Analyses were conducted using SPSS version 16.0 and SAS version 9.0. Means, standard deviations, skew, and kurtosis values are reported in Table 2. Variables with a kurtosis or skew value +/- 1.96 were considered kurtotic or skewed (Field, 2009). All dimensions were approximately normal, and visual inspection of the probability plots indicated linearity of the variables.

Reliability indices for dimension and domain scores across observations are reported in Table 3. Agreement calculations were computed by cycle, as the two 20-minute cycles are scored independently. Scores from the PWO analysis ranged from 53% to 100% for Cycle 1 and from 66% to 97% for Cycle 2.

Table 2

Means, Standard Deviations, Skew, and Kurtosis Values for CLASS Dimension Scores

Dimension	M	SD	Skew	Kurtosis
Positive Climate	5.60	.65	-1.02	1.61
Negative Climate	1.84	.67	.52	.49
Teacher Sensitivity	4.76	.98	-.37	-.18
Regard for Student Perspectives	4.91	.99	-.77	.49
Behavior Management	4.80	.84	-.34	-.37
Productivity	4.34	1.25	-.21	-.77
Instructional Learning Formats	4.02	1.24	-.23	-.68
Concept Development	3.30	1.18	.45	-.59
Quality of Feedback	3.99	1.17	-.05	-.70
Language Modeling	4.02	1.25	-.10	-1.07

Note. CLASS Pre-K scores range from 1 to 7.

Intraclass correlations are reported in Table 4. These correlations varied widely, ranging from .09 to .65 for Cycle 1 and from .20 to .65 for Cycle 2. Intraclass correlations for Positive Climate, Negative Climate, Instructional Learning Formats, Concept Development, and Quality of Feedback were statistically significant ($p <$ .05). Exact agreement had a broader range for Cycle 1 (6 - 66%) than for Cycle 2 (23 - 59%). Weighted *kappa* coefficients ranged from -.10 to .36 for Cycle 1 and from .01 to .32 for Cycle 2. Cohen's *kappa* coefficients ranged from -.15 to .27 for Cycle 1 and from -.12 to .33 for Cycle 2.

Discussion

The purpose of this study was to evaluate the interrater reliability of scores on the CLASS Pre-K observation scale for pre-kindergarten classrooms. Interrater reliability estimates of the scores were calculated and assessed through PWO analysis, intraclass correlations, exact agreement, weighted *kappa*, and Cohen's *kappa*. Results of this study indicated that interrater agreement using PWO criterion was comparable to the interrater agreement reported in the technical manual and previous research. The more stringent indices, however, were lower than those reported in previous CLASS Pre-K research (e.g., Howes et al., 2008; La Paro et al., 2004; Pianta et al., 2008).

Table 3

Interrater Agreement for CLASS Dimension and Domain Scores across Observations (N = 32)

Dimension	Percent Agreement				Kappa	
	+/-1		Exact		Weighted	Cohen's
	Cycle 1	Cycle 2	Cycle 1	Cycle 2	Combined Cycles	Combined Cycles
Positive Climate	100	97	66	59	.30	.21
Negative Climate	100	91	38	50	.19	.11
Teacher Sensitivity	75	75	38	34	.07	.05
Regard for Student Perspectives	84	72	25	23	.08	-.01
Behavior Management	88	88	44	44	.21	.16
Productivity	53	66	6	44	.30	.33
Instructional Learning Formats	75	78	31	31	.32	.18
Concept Development	69	69	25	25	.01	-.12
Quality of Feedback	72	81	31	34	.29	.11

(Table continues)

Language Modeling	69	81	38	25	.12	.02
Domain						
Emotional Support	90	84	41	41	-	-
Classroom Organization	72	77	27	40	-	-
Instructional Support	70	77	31	28	-	-

Table 4

Intraclass Correlations (ω²) for CLASS Dimensions across Observations (N = 32)

	Cycle 1	Cycle 2
Dimension	ω^2	ω^2
Positive Climate	.65*	.62*
Negative Climate	.31	.47*
Teacher Sensitivity	-.03	.20
Regard for Student Perspectives	.37	.37
Behavior Management	.14	.41
Productivity	.09	.45
Instructional Learning Formats	.51*	.62*
Concept Development	.44*	.42*
Quality of Feedback	.41*	.65*
Language Modeling	.35	.32

Note. $*p < .05$

The primary hypothesis of this study was that dimension and domain scores of the CLASS Pre-K would demonstrate adequate interrater reliability in a pre-kindergarten setting. Not surprisingly, scores from PWO analysis demonstrated the strongest agreement. Using the interpretive criteria outlined previously, one dimension (Productivity, Cycle 1) fell into the unacceptable range. PWO agreement percentages for Productivity, Concept Development, and Language Modeling fell in the marginally acceptable range. All other dimension percentages ranged from relatively acceptable to acceptable, with approximately half of the dimensions and one-third of the domains falling in the acceptable range. The Emotional Support domain (i.e., Positive Climate, Negative Climate, Teacher Sensitivity, and Regard for Student Perspectives) most frequently met the acceptable agreement criterion across all observations.

CLASS Pre-K scores also were examined through intraclass correlations and calculations of exact agreement. Intraclass correlations ranged from unacceptable to marginally reliable. When measured through exact agreement, estimates for the dimensions fell in the unacceptable range. The one exception was Positive Climate, which consistently had the highest rate of agreement for both intraclass correlations and exact agreement calculations. All of the *kappa* coefficients fell in the unacceptable range and some coefficients were slightly negative, indicating that levels of agreement did not differ from chance. The lower agreement percentages and *kappa* coefficients could be a reflection of the "authentic" observation conditions (i.e., raters completed real-time observations in the preschool classroom environment, rather than simulated observations via videotaped segments). The negative *kappa* coefficients may have occurred because most ratings, regardless of observer, fell within a small range (1 – 2 points) for multiple CLASS dimensions, increasing the likelihood of chance agreement.

Analyses conducted on CLASS Pre-K scores indicated that certain dimensions and domains consistently produced scores with higher reliability indices. The Emotional Support domain, particularly the Positive Climate and Negative Climate, demonstrated perfect reliability on certain cycles and generally had the highest reliability indices across all measures of agreement. When measured with a PWO analysis, all of the Emotional Support dimensions, with the exception of Teacher Sensitivity, had reliability indices that fell into the acceptable range.

The reliability indices for Classroom Organization and Instructional Support exhibited slightly lower agreement indices, with PWO agreements falling primarily into the relatively acceptable range. In the Classroom Organization domain, Behavior Management had the highest agreement indices, while Productivity demonstrated the lowest levels of agreement. The three dimensions (Concept Development, Quality of Feedback, and Language Modeling) that combined to form the Instructional Support domain displayed marginally reliable to acceptable levels of PWO agreement across both cycles.

The general structure of the real-time pre-kindergarten environments observed in this study may have negatively impacted the interrater reliability of scores on CLASS Pre-K. In particular, formal whole-group instructional time was fairly infrequent in participating classrooms, therefore limiting opportunities to observe rich examples of certain dimensions within the Instructional Support and Classroom Organization domains (e.g., Productivity, Concept Development). Conversely, participating classrooms provided ample opportunity to observe aspects of the Emotional Support domain (e.g., Positive Climate). Additionally, there were often multiple adults (e.g., instructional aides, student teachers) present in a classroom, assisting the primary teacher. Although the CLASS Pre-K manual instructs raters to weight behaviors across the adults in this situation (Pianta et al., 2008), the method relies on the subjective judgment of the rater, which is potentially problematic for interrater reliability. In addition, observers are not explicitly trained regarding the weighting of scores across adults during CLASS Pre-K certification training. Thus, CLASS Pre-K may yield more reliable estimates in pre-kindergarten classrooms if observations are completed primarily during formal whole-group instructional time conducted by the primary teacher. It may be important for new CLASS Pre-K users to spend additional time understanding and practicing Classroom Organization and Instructional Support domains, and coding in classrooms with multiple adults during training, before using the scale for research or practice.

Finally, when comparing CLASS Pre-K to the previously reviewed ECERS-R and the ELLCO scales, the Classroom Organization and Instructional Support domains demonstrated PWO agreement that was similar to that of the ECERS-R (i.e., .71; Harms et al., 1998). In addition, the PWO agreement for scores on the Emotional Support domain was equivalent to average interrater agreement for ELLCO scores (i.e., .90; Smith et al., 2008). As such, the domains scores for CLASS Pre-K exhibited PWO agreement similar to other widely used observation scales.

Directions for Future Research

There are several limitations that must be considered before conclusions can be drawn regarding these results. First, this study utilized a minimally sufficient sample of observations in classrooms that were all located in the same geographic area. The classroom teachers, as well as the observers, were relatively homogeneous across gender and race. Second, all pre-kindergarten classrooms were located in private schools, so the results may not generalize to all school settings. Third, data collectors were not assigned completely at random across classroom observations. Some pairs of data collectors observed together more than once, and some individuals observed the same classroom multiple times. Finally, the current study solely focused on one form of reliability evidence for CLASS Pre-K scores. While interrater reliability is an important psychometric property, examination of score validity is essential to justify use of scores from a measurement system such as CLASS Pre-K.

To address these limitations, future studies should include a larger and more heterogeneous sample of classrooms in private and public schools and randomly assign pairs of raters to those classrooms. Future research also should investigate the stability of the CLASS Pre-K ratings by examining the domain scores across successive observations in a classroom. The overall stability of the domains in each classroom would provide support for the use of CLASS Pre-K as an accurate "snapshot" of classroom quality. Finally, future studies should examine validity evidence (e.g., internal structure, relationships with other variables), as well as other types of reliability evidence (e.g., internal consistency, test-retest, etc.) for scores on the CLASS Pre-K with diverse populations to provide a comprehensive picture of the psychometric strengths and weaknesses of the observation scale.

Conclusion

The purpose of the current study was to evaluate the interrater reliability of CLASS Pre-K for real-time observations in a classroom setting. Among the multiple reliability indices considered within this study, PWO analysis demonstrated the highest level of agreement ($\geq$ .80) and this finding was consistent with previous research by authors of the CLASS Pre-K (La Paro et al., 2004; Howes et al., 2008; Pianta et al., 2008). The Emotional Support domain (i.e., Positive Climate, Negative Climate, Teacher Sensitivity, and Regard for Student Perspectives) had the highest rate of meeting the agreement criterion across all observations. The more stringent reliability indices demonstrated much lower levels of agreement, often falling into the less acceptable range.

CLASS Pre-K is an observation system that assesses the quality of an early childhood education environment. The use of CLASS Pre-K allows for educators to quantify specific, theoretically and empirically supported variables during a classroom observation (Pianta et al., 2008). As such, information obtained through this observation system could provide specific constructive feedback to teachers regarding empirically supported teaching practices. Before using this scale to gather information and potentially evoke change, users must establish consistency and accuracy.

In light of the findings from this initial study, more research is needed regarding the interrater reliability of scores on CLASS Pre-K for real-time observations in pre-kindergarten classrooms. Until such studies are completed, users should be cautious in their interpretation of CLASS Pre-K scores and supplement their observations with additional measures when making decisions regarding classroom quality.

References

Bronfenbrenner, U., & Morris, P. A. (1998). The ecology of developmental processes. In W. Damon & R. M. Lerner (Eds.), *Handbook of child psychology: Theoretical models of human development* (5th ed.) (pp. 993-1028). New York: John Wiley & Sons.

Buyse, E., Verschueren, K., & Doumen, S. (2011). Preschoolers' attachment to mother and risk for adjustment problems in kindergarten: Can teachers make a difference? *Social Development, 20*, 33-50. doi:10.1111/j.1467-9507.2009.00555.x

Cohen, J. (1960). A coefficient of agreement for nominal scales. *Educational and Psychological Measurement, 20*, 37-46. doi:10.1177/001316446002000104

Cohen, J. (1968). Weighted kappa: Nominal scale agreement with provision for scaled disagreement of partial credit. *Psychological Bulletin, 70*, 213-220. doi:10.1037/h0026256

Curby, T. W., Rimm-Kaufman, S. E., & Ponitz, C. C. (2009). Teacher-child interactions and children's achievement trajectories across kindergarten and first grade. *Journal of Educational Psychology, 101*, 912-925. doi:10.1037/a0016647

Douglas, F. (2004, September). *A critique of ECERS as a measure of quality in early childhood education and care.* Paper presented at 'Questions of Quality,' CECDE International Conference, Dublin Castle.

Field, A. (2009). *Discovering statistics using SPSS.* (3rd ed.). London: Sage.

Fleiss, J. L., & Cohen, J. (1973). The equivalence of weighted kappa and the intra-class correlation coefficient as measures of reliability. *Educational and Psychological Measurement, 33*, 613-619. doi: 10.1177/001316447303300309

Good, T. L., & Brophy, J. E. (2000). *Looking in classrooms* (8th ed.). New York: Longman.

Grinder, E. L. (2007). *Review of early childhood classroom observation measures.* Harrisburg: Pennsylvania's Departments of Education and Public Welfare.

Gwet, K. (2002). Kappa statistic is not satisfactory for assessing the extent of agreement between raters. *Statistical Methods for Inter-Rater Reliability Assessment, 1*, 1-6.

Hamre, B. K., Goffin, S. G., & Kraft-Sayre, M. (2009). *Classroom Assessment Scoring System implementation guide: Measuring and improving classroom interactions in early childhood settings.* Center for Advanced Study of Teaching and Learning. Retrieved from *http://curry.virginia.edu/research/centers/castl/publications*

Hamre, B. K., Justice, L. M., Pianta, R. C., Kilday, C., Sweeney, B., Downer, J. T., & Leach, A. (2010). Implementation fidelity of MyTeachingPartner literacy and language activities: Association with preschoolers' language and literacy growth. *Early Childhood Research Quarterly, 25*, 329-347. doi:10.1016/j. ecresq.2009.07.002

Hamre, K. B., Mashburn, A. J., Pianta, R. C., & Locasle-Crouch, J. (2008). *Classroom Assessment Scoring System, Pre-K: Technical appendix*, Baltimore, MD: Paul H. Brookes Publishing Co.

Hamre, K. B., & Pianta, R. C. (2005). Can instructional and emotional support in the first grade make a difference for children at risk of school failure? *Child Development, 76*, 949-967. doi: 10.1111/j.1467-8624.2005.00889.x

Harms, T., Clifford, R. M., & Cryer, D. (1998). *Early Childhood Environment Rating Scale-Revised.* New York, NY: Teachers College Press.

Howes, C., Burchinal, M., Pianta, R. C., Bryant, D., Early, D., & Clifford, R. R. (2008). Ready to learn? Children's pre-academic achievement in pre-kindergarten programs. *Early Childhood Research Quarterly, 23*, 27-50. doi: 10.1016/j.ecresq.2007.05.002

La Paro, K. M., & Pianta, R. C. (2000). Predicting children's competence in the early school years: A meta-analytic review. *Review of Educational Research, 70*, 443-484. doi:10.1016/j.jsp.2006.01.003

La Paro, K. M., Pianta, R., C., & Stuhlman, M. (2004). The Classroom Assessment Scoring System: Findings from the pre-kindergarten year. *The Elementary School Journal, 104*, 409-426. doi: 10.1086/499760

Malmberg, L., Hagger, H., Burn, K., Mutton, T., & Colls, H. (2010). Observed classroom quality during teacher education and two years of professional practice. *Journal of Educational Psychology, 102*, 916-932. doi:10.1037/a0020920

Nelson, K. P., Edwards, D., Gamishev, T., & Kozarev, R. (2007). *On population-based measures of agreement.* Retrieved from http://130.203.133.150/viewdoc/summary?doi=10.1.1.74.5381

Nunnally, J., & Bernstein, I. (1994). *Psychometric Theory* (3rd ed.). New York: McGraw Hill.

Olswang, L. B., Svensson, L., Coggins, T. E., Beilinson, J. S., & Donalson, A., L. (2006). Reliability issues and solutions for coding social communication performance in classroom settings. *Journal of Speech, Language, and Hearing Research, 49,* 1958-1068. doi:10.1044/1092-4388 (2006/075)

Pakarinen, E., Kiuru, N., Lerkkanen, M., Poikkeus, A., Ahonen, T., & Nurmi, J. (2010). Instructional support predicts children's task avoidance in kindergarten. *Early Childhood Research Quarterly, 26,* 376-386. doi: 10.1016/j. ecresq.2010.11.003

Perlman, M., Zellman, G. L., & Vi-Nhuan, L. (2004). Examining the psycho-metric properties of the Early Childhood Environment Rating Scale-Revised (ECERS-R). *Early Childhood Research Quarterly, 19*, 398-412. doi: 10.1016/j.ecresq.2004.07.006

Pianta, R. C. (1999). *Enhancing relationships between children and teachers.* Washington, DC: American Psychological Association. doi: 10.1037/10314-000

Pianta, R. C., La Paro, K. M., & Hamre, B. K. (2008). *Classroom Assessment Scoring System, Pre-k.* Baltimore, MD: Paul H. Brookes Publishing Co.

Pianta, R. C., La Paro, K. M., Payne, C., Cox, M. J., & Bradley, R. (2002). The relationship of kindergarten classroom environment to teacher, family, and school characteristics and child outcomes. *Elementary School Journal, 102*, 225-238. doi:10.1086/499701

Rimm-Kaufman, S. E., & Chiu, Y. J. (2007). Promoting social and academic competence in the classroom. *Psychology in the Schools, 44*, 397-413. doi: 10.1002/pits.20231

Rimm-Kaufman, S. E., Curby, T. W., Grimm, K. J., Nathanson, L., & Brock, L. L. (2009). The contribution of children's self-regulation and classroom quality to children's adaptive behaviors in the kindergarten classroom. *Developmental Psychology, 45*, 958-972. doi:10.1037/a0015861

Rutter, M., & Maughan, B. (2002). School effectiveness findings, 1979-2002. *Journal of School Psychology, 40*, 451-475. doi:10.1016/S0022-4405(02)00124-3

Salvia, J., & Ysseldyke, J. E. (2007). *Assessment in Special and Inclusive Education.* (10th ed.). New York: Houghton Mifflin Company.

Sandefur, J. T., & Bressler, A. A. (1970). *Classroom observation systems in preparing school personnel.* Washington, DC: U.S. Department of Health, Education and Welfare. (ERIC Document Reproduction Service No. ED 037377).

Sattler, J. (2001). *Assessment of Children: Cognitive Applications* (4th ed.). San Diego: Jerome Sattler, Publisher, Inc.

Shrout, P. E., & Fleiss, J. L. (1979). Intraclass correlations: Uses in assessing rater reliability. *Psychological Bulletin, 86*, 420-428. doi:10.1037/0033-2909.86.2.420

Smith, M. W., Brady, J. P., & Clark-Chiarelli, N. (2008). *User's guide to the Early Language and Literacy Classroom Observation K-3 Tool* (Research ed.). Baltimore, MD: Paul H. Brookes Publishing Co.

Smith, M. W., & Dickinson, D. K. (2002). *User's guide to the Early Language and Literacy Classroom Observation toolkit.* Baltimore, MD: Paul H. Brookes Publishing Co.

Suen, H. K. (1988). Agreement, reliability, accuracy, and validity: Toward a clarification. *Behavioral Assessment, 10*, 343-366.

U.S. Department of Health and Human Services, Administration for Children and Families, Early Childhood Learning and Knowledge Center (2008). *Classroom Assessment Scoring System* (Log No. ACF-IM-HS-08-11). Retrieved from http://eclkc.ohs.acf.hhs.gov/hslc/resources/Professional%20Development/Staff%20Development/Teaching%20Teams/resour_ime_011_0081908.html

Wood, J. M. (2007). Understanding and computing Cohen's kappa: A tutorial. *WebPsychEmpiricist*. Retrieved from http://wpe.info/papers_table.html.

Syndromes of Preschool Psychopathology Reported by Teachers and Caregivers in 14 Societies Using the Caregiver-Teacher Report Form (C-TRF)

Masha Y. Ivanova
University of Vermont

Thomas M. Achenbach
University of Vermont

Leslie A. Rescorla
Bryn Mawr College

Niels Bilenberg
University of Southern Denmark

Gudrun Bjarnadottir
Glaesibaer & Arbaer
Health Clinics

Silvia Denner
Dortmund University of
Applied Social Sciences

Pedro Dias
Catholic University of Portugal

Anca Dobrean
Babes-Bolyai University

Manfred Doepfner
University
of
Cologne

Elaheh Mohammad
Esmaeili
Research Institute
for Education

Alessandra Frigerio
Scientific Institute E. Medea

Halldor S. Gudmundsson
University of Iceland

Roma Jusiene
Vilnius University

Solvejg Kristensen
University of Southern Denmark

Felipe Lecannelier
Universidad del Desarrollo

Patrick W.L. Leung
Chinese University of Hong Kong

Vânia Sousa Lima
Catholic University of Portugal

Jianghong Liu
University of Pennsylvania

Sofia P. Lobel
Universidad del Desarrollo

Bárbara César Machado
Catholic University of Portugal

Jasminka Markovic
Institute of Psychiatry,
Clinical Center of Vojvodina

Paola A. Mas
Universidad
del Desarrollo

Rosario Montirosso
Scientific Institute E. Medea

Julia Plueck,
University of Cologne

Adelina A. Pronaj
University Clinical Center of Kosovo

Jorge T. Rodriguez,
Universidad del Desarrollo

Pamela O. Rojas,
Universidad del Desarrollo

Klaus Schmeck,
Psychiatric University Hospitals Basel

Mimoza Shahini
University Clinical Center of Kosovo

Jaime R. Silva
Universidad de La Frontera

Jan van der Ende
Erasmus University
Medical Center-Sophia Children's
Hospital

Frank C. Verhulst
Erasmus University
Medical Center-Sophia Children's
Hospital

Caregivers and teachers from 14 societies rated 9,389 1.5 to 5-year-olds
on the Caregiver-Teacher Report Form (C-TRF; Achenbach & Rescorla,
2000). General population samples were obtained in Asia; the Middle
East; Eastern, Northern, Central, Western, and Southern Europe; and
South America. The 2-level 6-syndrome C-TRF model derived on a
mostly U.S. sample was tested separately for each society. This model
or a slightly modified 2-level 5-syndrome version of the model fit the
data for 10 of the 14 societies. The findings generally support use of
the C-TRF with children of diverse backgrounds. The multicultural
generalizability of C-TRF syndromes suggests that they can be used
as taxonomic constructs for preschoolers' psychopathology, which can
facilitate international communication and collaboration between clinicians, researchers, and educators working with young children.

It is now widely recognized that very young children can experience significant
emotional and behavioral problems, and that these problems should not be ignored.
A recent editorial in a leading child and adolescent psychiatry journal proclaimed
that the field of preschool mental health "has arrived – on a global scale" (Carter,
2010, p. 1181).

Reliable and valid assessment instruments are needed to aid in the identification
and treatment of psychopathology in young children. Most mental health instru-

ments designed for the assessment of preschoolers use parents' reports. However, in the United States (U.S.), the majority of preschoolers spend a significant amount of time in the care of persons other than their parents. The U.S. Census Bureau estimates that over 60% of U.S. children between the ages of zero and six receive regular childcare from persons other than their parents (Federal Interagency Forum on Child and Family Statistics, 2010). This percentage would be substantially higher if the age range excluded infancy. As more women enter the workforce in response to economic globalization and recession, non-parental childcare arrangements will become more prevalent around the globe. Consequently, reliable and valid assessment instruments using non-parental caregiver (e.g., daycare providers, nannies) and teacher reports will be increasingly important for the assessment of preschoolers.

Several standardized instruments that use caregiver or teacher reports are available for assessing the emotional, behavioral, and social functioning of preschoolers. These include the Conners' Teacher Rating Scale (CTRS; Conners, 1997); Childcare Provider Form of the Infant Toddler Social Emotional Assessment (ITSEA; Carter & Briggs-Gowan, 2006), Preschool Behavior Questionnaire (PBQ; Behar & Stringfield, 1974), Social Competence and Behavior Evaluation Inventory (SCBE-30; LaFreniere & Dumas, 1996), Strengths and Difficulties Questionnaire for Educators of 3- and 4-Year-Old Children (SDQ T/3-4; Goodman, 1997; Koglen, Barquero, Mayer, Scheithaur, & Petermann, 2007), and the Caregiver-Teacher Report Form (C-TRF; Achenbach & Rescorla, 2000). All six of these instruments are paper-and-pencil questionnaires.

Because world communities are becoming more and more diverse, caregivers and teachers are dealing with more cultural and ethnic differences among the children they serve. Consequently, instruments are needed for assessing preschoolers from diverse societies. However, a crucial question is whether an instrument measures the same constructs in different societies.

If an instrument is applied to general population samples in different societies, multivariate statistical analyses could be used to determine whether similar patterns of problems are found in the different societies. Statistically-derived patterns of co-occurring problems can be viewed as "syndromes." Such syndromes are often derived via factor analytic methods, which can be broadly grouped into exploratory and confirmatory factor analysis (EFA and CFA, respectively). EFA identifies syndromes of co-occurring problems, while CFA tests how well particular hypothesized syndromes fit the data. By testing syndromes in different societies, we can determine whether the same syndrome constructs apply in the different societies.

Correspondence concerning this article should be addressed to Masha Y. Ivanova, Ph.D., Department of Psychiatry, University of Vermont, 1 South Prospect Street, Burlington, VT 05401. E-mail: Masha.Ivanova@uvm.edu

The C-TRF obtains ratings of 99 emotional, behavioral, and social problems (plus one open-ended item) from caregivers and teachers of 18- through 71-month-old children. Achenbach and Rescorla (2000) derived six syndromes from C-TRF ratings of 1,113 mostly U.S. preschoolers. The six syndromes are designated as Emotionally Reactive, Anxious/Depressed, Somatic Complaints, Withdrawn, Attention Problems, and Aggressive Behavior. Second-order factor analyses showed that the first four and the last two syndromes form superordinate groupings labeled Internalizing and Externalizing, respectively.

Identification of syndromes that are common across societies can facilitate international collaboration among educators, clinicians, and researchers working with preschoolers. Despite the power of such an approach, few studies have examined syndrome structures of preschool psychopathology beyond the samples on which the assessment instruments were developed.

Syndromes Found in Caregiver/Teacher Ratings of Ethnically Diverse U.S. and Non-U.S. Samples

Two studies have tested the syndrome structures of caregiver/teacher-reported preschool psychopathology with ethnically diverse U.S. samples. To test the 3-syndrome structure of the PBQ, Johnson, Gomez, and Sanders-Phillips (1999) randomly selected San Diego Head Start teachers to rate 304 mostly Latino and African American 3- and 4-year-olds. A variety of EFAs failed to support Behar and Stringfield's (1974) Hostile-Aggressive, Anxious, and Hyperactive syndrome structure, but yielded two syndromes designated as Aggressive-Hyperactive-Distractible and Anxious-Fearful.

Gerhardstein, Lonigan, Cukrowicz, and McGuffey (2003) tested the generalizability of the CTRS syndrome model (Conners 1989; 1997) in a predominantly African American sample of 235 preschoolers. A hybrid CTRS comprising the 28 revised short form items (Conners, 1997) plus the 16 non-overlapping items from the original short form (Conners, 1989) was completed by teachers and research assistants. Various EFAs on both teacher ratings and ratings averaged across informants were performed on the 28 items and then all 44 items. The same results emerged across different types of analyses and item groups: The derived three-syndrome structure (Hyperactivity/Impulsivity, Inattention, and Oppositional Behavior) did not correspond to the syndrome structure of the Conners' (1997) revised short form (Oppositional, Cognitive Problems and Hyperactivity), but generally replicated the syndrome structure for the original Conners' short form (Hyperactivity, Inattentive/Passive, and Conduct Problems; Conners, 1989).

Three other studies tested the syndrome structures of caregiver/teacher-reported preschool psychopathology in non-U.S. samples. Rubin, Moller, and Emptage (1987) administered the PBQ to teachers of 157 Canadian first-graders. EFA yielded a 3-syndrome structure that was similar to Behar and Stringfield's (1974) original 3-syndrome solution. Rubin et al. concluded that, "Hostility/Aggression, Hyperactivity/Distractibility, and Anxiety/Fearfulness were, for the most part, defined by the same items that comprised these factors in Behar and Stringfield's original report" (p. 91).

Liu, Cheng, and Leung (2010) conducted the only study prior to the present study that tested the generalizability of the C-TRF 6-syndrome structure outside the U.S. Preschool teachers of 876 4- and 5-year-olds drawn from a population-based community cohort in the mainland Chinese city of Jintan completed a Chinese translation of the C-TRF. Using Achenbach and Rescorla's (2000) CFA procedures, Liu et al. tested two models: a one-factor model in which all items loaded on a single syndrome, and the 2-level 6-syndrome U.S. model with six first-order syndromes (Emotionally Reactive, Anxious/Depressed, Somatic Complaints, Withdrawn, Attention Problems, and Aggressive Behavior), plus second-order Internalizing and Externalizing groupings. The first model did not fit the data, but the second model achieved acceptable fit.

Finally, LaFreniere et al. (2002) conducted the only study to date that tested the syndrome structure of caregiver/teacher-reported preschool psychopathology across multiple societies. The SCBE-30 (LaFreniere & Dumas, 1996) was completed by caregivers or teachers of 4,640 3- to 6-year-olds attending urban daycare programs in Austria, Brazil, Canada, China, Italy, Japan, Russia, and the U.S. Principal components analysis with varimax rotation, which was applied separately to each data set, indicated the same three factor solution (i.e., social competence, anger-aggression, and anxiety-withdrawal) for each society.

Because LaFreniere et al. (2002) applied the same assessment methods and data analytic procedures across a range of societies, their results permit conclusions to be drawn about the generalizability of the SCBE-30 syndrome structure across the tested societies. However, since the other reviewed studies tested models in single cultural groups, applied different factor analytic methodologies to different assessment instruments, and tested instruments differing in content, they offer limited information about the generalizability of syndrome structures of preschool psychopathology to different ethnic groups and societies.

Purposes of the Present Study

As shown by LaFreniere et al. (2002), to advance our understanding of syndromes of caregiver/teacher-reported preschool psychopathology across ethnically and culturally diverse groups, we need to test syndrome models with assessment and analytic procedures that are standardized across a large number of societies. The purpose of the present study was to provide a multicultural test of syndromes of caregiver/teacher reported preschool psychopathology using standardized methodology across diverse societies. We tested whether C-TRF ratings of a broad range of emotional, behavioral, and social problems in 14 societies fit the syndrome structure previously found for Anglophone children mainly from the U.S. The 14 societies were located in Asia; the Middle East; Eastern, Northern, Central, Western, and Southern Europe; and South America.

Method

Samples

The second and third authors contacted indigenous investigators of emotional and behavioral problems in early childhood who assessed non-U.S. epidemiological samples using the C-TRF, and requested access to their data for multicultural comparisons. C-TRF ratings provided by caregivers/teachers from Austria, Chile, China, Denmark, Germany, Iceland, Iran, Italy, Kosovo, Lithuania, the Netherlands, Portugal, Romania, and Serbia for 9,389 1.5- to 5-year-old children were analyzed.

The sample had the following age composition: age 1½ to 2 (4%), age 2 (12%), age 3 (18%), age 4 (26%), and age 5 (40%). Respondents completed the C-TRF in their native languages. Table 1 presents sample sizes, primary references, proportions of boys, sampling frames, and recruitment procedures for the samples (Rescorla et al. [2011] used the same 14 samples, plus a U.S. general population sample in their companion paper reporting comparisons of distributions of the C-TRF scale scores). Sample sizes ranged from 299 (Iceland) to 1,350 (Iran). The sampling frame was national in 4 societies and regional in 10 societies. Recruitment procedures were household-based in 2 societies and school-based in 12 societies. The samples had about equal proportions of boys and girls. Children who had been referred for mental health or special education services in the preceding 12 months were excluded from the Italian sample before we received the data. Information about inclusion of children referred for mental health or special education services was not provided for most of the other societies. In each society, conventions for obtaining informed consent required by the investigator's research institution were followed. Based on procedures used in norming the C-TRF (Achenbach & Rescorla, 2000), children were excluded from analyses if ratings were missing for more than 8 items, with 0% of cases excluded for 5 societies, $\leq 1\%$ of cases excluded for 5 societies, 2% excluded for 1 society, and 6-7% excluded for 3 societies.

Tested Model

As Figure 1 illustrates, the 2-level U.S. model comprising the six correlated C-TRF first-order syndromes (Emotionally Reactive, Anxious/Depressed, Somatic Complaints, Withdrawn, Attention Problems, and Aggressive Behavior) plus the second-order Internalizing and Externalizing groupings was tested. The Internalizing and Externalizing groupings comprise the first four and last two first-order syndromes, respectively. Each of the 66 items comprising the first-order syndromes

Table 1

Sources of Data for Confirmatory Factor Analyses of the Caregiver-Teacher Report Form (C-TRF) in 14 Societies

Society (N)	Reference	% Male	Sampling frame	Recruitment
Austria (342)	Schmeck & Skrabel, 2004	52%	regional	school-based
Chile (848)	Lecannelier, 2011	54%	regional	school-based
China (931)	Liu et al., 2010	53%	regional	school-based
Denmark (625)	Kristensen et al., 2010	49%	regional	household
Germany (1237)	Denner & Schmeck, 2005; Doepfner & Plueck, 2009	52%	regional	school-based
Iceland (299)	Gudmundsson & Bjarnadottir, 2009	49%	national	school-based
Iran (1350)	Esmaeili, 2009	49%	national	school-based
Italy (526)	Frigerio et al., 2006	52%	regional	school-based
Kosovo (322)	Pronaj & Shahini, 2010	52%	regional	school-based
Lithuania (824)	Jusiene et al., 2007	53%	national	school-based
Netherlands (371)	Tick et al., 2007	52%	regional	household
Portugal (384)	Dias et al., 2009	51%	regional	school-based
Romania (953)	Dobrean et al., 2008	48%	national	school-based
Serbia (377)	Markovic, 2010	43%	regional	school-based

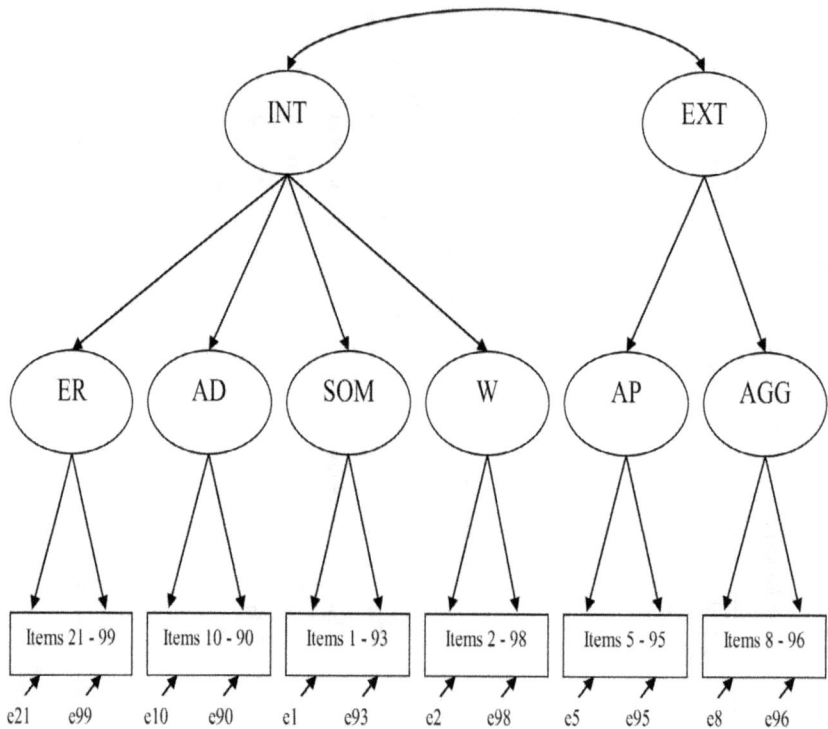

Figure 1. ER – Emotionally Reactive, AD – Anxious/Depressed, SC – Somatic Complaints, W – Withdrawn, AP – Attention Problems, AB – Aggressive Behavior, INT – Internalizing, EXT – Externalizing. All latent factors were correlated. Item numbers indicate items with the lowest and highest numbers on C-TRF syndromes.

was assigned to only one syndrome. For each first-order syndrome, we set one item's loading to 1.0 to identify the metric for that syndrome. All latent variables were allowed to be correlated and all item residuals were uncorrelated, which are the default settings in the statistical program we used (Mplus 6.0; Muthen & Muthen, 2009).

Data Analysis

Caregivers/teachers rated the C-TRF items as *0 = not true (as far as you know)*, *1 = somewhat or sometimes true*, and *2 = very true or often true*, based on the preceding 2 months. The weighted least squares with standard errors and mean- and variance-adjusted χ^2 estimator (WLSMV) via Mplus 6.0 (Muthen & Muthen, 2009) was used to account for the non-normal distribution of the data. To avoid excessively small cell sizes, items were dichotomized as 0 versus 1 or 2. Associations between items were then quantified via tetrachoric correlations. The Root Mean Square Error of Approximation (RMSEA) was used as the primary index of model fit, as Yu and Muthen (2002) concluded that it was the best model fit index for the WLSMV, based on the results of their Monte Carlo study. The RMSEA cutoff of .06 was used to indicate good fit, as Yu and Muthen (2002) concluded that a cutoff of about .05 to .06 should be used with categorical variables. The RMSEA cutoff of .08 was used to indicate acceptable fit (Browne & Cudeck, 1993). To follow the convention of using multiple model fit indices, the Comparative Fit Index (CFI; Bentler, 1990) and the Tucker-Lewis Index (TLI; Tucker. & Lewis, 1973) were also computed, but were regarded as secondary. For CFI and TLI, Hu and Bentler (1999) proposed values > .95 for good model fit. However, Marsh, Hau, and Wen (2004) criticized Hu and Bentler's criterion as being excessively conservative because it rejected correctly specified complex models. Since the current models were complex, the criteria of >.90 for good fit and .80 to .90 for acceptable fit were used, as recommended by Browne and Cudeck (1993).

Results

CFAs of the 2-level 6-syndrome U.S. model

The model illustrated in Figure 1 converged for all samples. As shown in Table 2, RMSEAs indicated good model fit for all societies, ranging from .030 (Denmark) to .060 (Germany). CFI and TLI results were generally consistent with RMSEA results. However, for all societies except China and Portugal, Mplus produced a warning that the latent variable variance/covariance matrix (PSI) was non-positive definite. Such a warning indicates potential problems with model identification and should be investigated. Possible causes of non-positive definiteness include out-of-range parameters (i.e., a negative variance or residual variance for a latent variable, a correlation ≥ 1.0 between two latent variables), and a linear dependency among more than two latent variables (Muthen & Muthen, 2009).

CFA solutions for the 12 societies with the warning pointed to high correlations between the Emotionally Reactive and Anxious/Depressed latent variables (.72 to .96) as potential causes of the non-positive definite PSI matrices. When the model was rerun with these latent variables combined, the PSI matrix problem was resolved for 8 of the 12 societies (Austria, Denmark, Germany, Iceland, Italy, the Netherlands, Romania, and Serbia).

Additional CFAs for Chile, Iran, Kosovo, and Lithuania

A less differentiated model of emotional and behavioral problems was tested for the four societies for which combining the Emotionally Reactive and Anx-

Table 2

Results of Confirmatory Factor Analyses

Society (N)	Two-Level 6-Factor U.S. Model			Two-Level U.S. Model with ER and AD Factors Combined		
	RMSEA	CFI	TLI	RMSEA	CFI	TLI
Austria (342)	.036[a]	.854	.849	.036	.850	.845
Chile (848)	.053[a]	.880	.876	.054[a]	.878	.874
China (931)	.044	.833	.827	[b]	[b]	[b]
Denmark (625)	.030[a]	.912	.909	.030	.912	.909
Germany (1237)	.060[a]	.832	.826	.061	.824	.818
Iceland (299)	.031[a.]	.896	.892	.031	.895	.892
Iran (1350)	.059[a]	.788	.781	.060[a]	.785	.778
Italy (526)	.046[a]	.845	.840	.046	.847	.841
Kosovo (322)	.045[a]	.865	.860	.045[a]	.864	.859
Lithuania (824)	.054[a]	.820	.814	.055[a]	.815	.809
Netherlands (371)	038[a]	.881	.877	.039	.877	.873
Portugal (384)	.038	.872	.868	[b]	[b]	[b]
Romania (953)	.054[a]	.813	.807	.054	.813	.806
Serbia (377)	.049[a]	.865	.861	.049	.865	.861

Note. RMSEA = Root Mean Square Error of Approximation; CFI = Comparative Fit Index; TLI = Tucker-Lewis Index; ER = Emotionally Reactive syndrome; AD = Anxious/Depressed syndrome.
[a]The PSI matrix is not positive definite.
[b]Because Mplus produced no warnings for China and Portugal, their data were not tested with the ER and AD factors combined.

ious/Depressed syndromes did not resolve the PSI matrix problem. Specifically, a first-order, 2-factor model in which items comprising the Emotionally Reactive, Anxious/Depressed, Withdrawn, and Somatic Complaints syndromes were assigned to the Internalizing factor, while items comprising the Attention Problems and Aggressive Behavior syndromes were assigned to the Externalizing factor was tested for Chile, Iran, Kosovo, and Lithuania. The fit of this first-order 2-factor model was acceptable for Iran (RMSEA = .063) and good for Chile, Kosovo, and Lithuania (RMSEAs = .057, .046, and .057, respectively).

Out-of-range parameters

For both 6- and 5-syndrome, 2-level models that were tested, one item loading was out-of-range for Iceland (86. *Too concerned with neatness and cleanliness*), Portugal (45. *Nausea, feels sick without medical cause*), and Serbia (93. *Vomiting, throwing up without medical cause*). As recommended by Chen et al. (2001) and McDonald (2004), VanDriel's technique (1978) was used to test these loadings. VanDriel recommended testing out-of-range parameters by forming confidence intervals around them and determining whether the confidence intervals overlapped with the admissible parameter space. In the case of an overlap, the out-of-range parameter estimate could be attributable to sampling fluctuations. The 95% confidence intervals around the out-of-range parameters contained admissable parameter values for all three item loadings.

Discussion

The present study provided a multicultural test of syndromes of caregiver and teacher reported preschool psychopathology using standardized assessment and data analytic procedures across 14 societies. We tested how well a 2-level, 6-syndrome model derived for the C-TRF from a mostly U.S. sample would fit caregiver and teacher ratings of preschool children from societies very different from the U.S. We found that the 2-level, 6-syndrome U.S. model produced acceptable to good model fit indices for all societies, except Iran. However, for Austria, Chile, Denmark, Germany, Iceland, Iran, Italy, Kosovo, Lithuania, the Netherlands, Romania, and Serbia, CFAs of the 2-level 6-syndrome model produced warnings indicating potential model specification problems. Because CFA solutions identified high correlations between the Emotionally Reactive and Anxious/Depressed latent variables as possible reasons for the warnings, these syndromes were combined and a 2-level 5-syndrome model was tested for the 12 societies. For all societies, except Chile, Iran, Kosovo, and Lithuania, the 2-level 5-syndrome model converged without warnings and fit the data well. Additional CFAs of a first-order 2-factor model comprising the Internalizing and Externalizing syndromes indicated acceptable model fit for Iran and good model fit for Chile, Kosovo, and Lithuania.

The Emotionally Reactive and Anxious/Depressed latent variables were also highly correlated in the U.S. general population sample that was used by Rescorla et al. (2011) in the companion paper ($r = .83$). However, the correlation between the observed scale scores, which include measurement error and which may be of particular relevance to assessment of individual children, was substantially lower ($r = .69$).

The results indicated that caregiver and teacher ratings of a broad range of problems generally fit the syndrome structure previously found for a mainly U.S. sample. However, our findings raised questions about whether the Emotionally

Reactive and Anxious/Depressed syndromes are clearly separable in all the tested societies.

The generalizability of C-TRF syndromes across most of the tested societies indicates that we can meaningfully compare scores on most of the C-TRF syndrome scales between the tested societies. In a companion study, Rescorla et al. (2011) compared scores on C-TRF syndrome scales for the 14 samples used in the present study, plus the U.S. general population sample. Variance within societies greatly exceeded variance between societies, and the effect sizes for differences among the 15 societies were in the small to medium range, according to Cohen's (1988) criteria. On a scale that could range from 0 to 198, 10 of the 15 societies had mean scores within 8.6 points (1 SD) of the omnicultural mean (the mean of all means). The results of the present study are consistent with findings for parent ratings of preschoolers' emotional, behavioral, and social problems on a parent-report counterpart to the C-TRF, the Child Behavior Checklist for Ages 1.5-5 (CBCL/1.5-5; Achenbach & Rescorla, 2000). Ivanova et al. (2010) tested the fit of the CBCL/1.5-5 7-syndrome model using ratings by 19,106 parents from 23 societies located in Asia, Australasia, Europe, the Middle East, and South America. The CBCL/1.5-5 syndrome model comprises the six syndromes it shares with the C-TRF, plus a syndrome designated as Sleep Problems. CFAs indicated acceptable to good fit of the tested model in all societies. Like the present study, Ivanova et al. (2010) also found high correlations between the Emotionally Reactive and Anxious/Depressed latent factors that created model strain.

Implications and Limitations

Taken together, the results of the present study and the Ivanova et al. (2010) study indicate that C-TRF and CBCL/1.5-5 syndromes are generalizable across many very different societies. This suggests that the syndromes can serve as taxonomic constructs of preschoolers' psychopathology reported by parents and caregivers/teachers in the tested societies. The syndromes can aid professionals working with preschool children in conceptualizing the emotional, behavioral, and social problems of preschoolers in various societies. The syndromes can also be used to facilitate communication and collaboration between clinicians, educators, and researchers working with preschoolers around the world.

Because we could not include data from all human societies in this or the Ivanova et al. (2010) study, the C-TRF and CBCL/1.5-5 syndromes should be used with caution in societies in which the syndromes were not tested. The C-TRF syndromes should also be used with caution in Chile, Iran, Kosovo, and Lithuania because CFAs of the tested U.S. syndrome model produced potentially serious warnings. Our results indicated that a less differentiated model comprising the Internalizing and Externalizing groupings can be used in Chile, Iran, Kosovo, and Lithuania with confidence.

Societies differ greatly in the proportions of children enrolled in daycare and preschool, in selective factors related to which children are enrolled, in the nature of the programs, and in the training of caregivers and preschool teachers. These differences may contribute to the greater variations in C-TRF syndromal patterns than have been found in parent ratings of preschoolers and in parent, teacher, and self-ratings of older children (Ivanova et al., 2007a, b, c; 2010).

Other limitations of the present study include the possibility that additional syndrome models might fit the data, and a lack of definitive criteria for model fit indices (i.e., it is still being debated which cut off criteria for which model fit indices should be used under which conditions). Furthermore, the 66 items of the C-TRF syndromes may not capture all emotional, behavioral, and social problems (e.g., Autism Spectrum Disorders) that are important to caregivers and teachers working with preschool children in all societies. However, the 99 items of the C-TRF and CBCL/1.5-5 are also scored on the following DSM-oriented scales that are based on clinical judgments by an international panel of experts: Affective Problems, Anxiety Problems, Pervasive Developmental Problems, Attention Deficit/Hyper-activity Problems, and Oppositional Defiant Problems. Some of these scales have been found to be significantly associated with diagnoses such as Autism Spectrum Disorders (Muratori et al., 2008; Sikora et al., 2008). Another limitation of our study was that sample sizes were relatively small for a few societies. It is possible that the one out-of-range item loadings found for Iceland, Portugal, and Serbia was due to insufficient item variance in their relatively small samples of 299, 384, and 377, respectively.

In summary, the results of the present study support use of the C-TRF with children of diverse backgrounds by demonstrating that C-TRF syndromes gener-ally capture patterns of emotional, behavioral, and social problems in caregiver and teacher ratings of preschoolers in many societies. The C-TRF syndromes thus demonstrated considerable similarity among patterns of caregiver and teacher rat-ings from societies in Asia; the Middle East; Eastern, Northern, Central, Western, and Southern Europe; and South America. The C-TRF and CBCL/1.5-5 offer mental health professionals and educators efficient and easy-to-use tools for multi-informant assessment of preschoolers of diverse cultural backgrounds.

References

Achenbach, T. M., & Rescorla, L.A. (2000). *Manual for the ASEBA preschool forms and profiles.* Burlington, VT: University of Vermont, Department of Psychiatry.

Behar, L., & Stringfield, S. (1974). A behavior ratings scale for the preschool child. *Developmental Psychology, 10,* 601-610.

Bentler, P. M. (1990). Comparative fit indices in structural models. *Psychological Bulletin,107,* 238-246. doi: 10.1037/0033-2909.107.2.238

Browne, M. W., & Cudeck, R. (1993). Alternative ways of assessing model fit. In K. A. Bollen & J. S. Long (Eds.), *Testing structural equation models* (pp. 136-162). Newbury Park, CA: Sage.

Carter, A. (2010). The field of toddler/preschool mental health has arrived – on a global scale. *Journal of the American Academy of Child and Adolescent Psychiatry, 49,* 1181-1182. doi: 10.1016/j.jaac.2010.09.006

Carter, A. S., & Briggs-Gowan, M. J. (2006). *The Infant-Toddler Social & Emotional Assessment (ITSEA).* San Antonio, Texas: Psychological Corporation, Harcourt Assessment.

Chen, F., Bollen, K. A., Paxton, P., Curran, P. J., & Kirby, J. B. (2001). Improper solutions in structural equation models. *Sociological Methods and Research, 29,* 468-508. doi: 10.1177/0049124101029004003

Cohen, J. (1988). *Statistical power analysis for the behavioral sciences* (2nd ed.). New York: Academic Press.

Conners, C. K. (1989). *Conners' Rating Scale – Revised.* North Tonawanda, NY: Multi-Health Systems.

Conners, C. K. (1997). *Conners' Rating Scale – Revised.* North Tonawanda, NY: Multi-Health Systems.

Denner, S., & Schmeck, K. (2005). Emotional and behavioural disorders at preschool age –results of a study in kindergarten children in Dortmund using the Caregiver-Teacher Report Form C-TRF/1½ –5. *Zeitschrift für Kinder- und Jugendpsychiatrie und Psychotherapie, 33,* 307–317.

Dias, P., Machado, B., Silva, J., & Goncalves, M. (2009). [Child Behavior Checklist/1½-5 and C-TRF scores for Portuguese preschool children]. Unpublished raw data.

Dobrean, A. (2008). [Child Behavior Checklist/1.5-5 and C-TRF scores for Romanian preschool children]. Unpublished raw data.

Doepfner, M., & Plueck, J. (2009). [Child Behavior Checklist/1½-5 and C-TRF scores for German preschool children]. Unpublished raw data.

Esmaeili, E. M. (2009). [Child Behavior Checklist/1½-5 and C-TRF scores for Iranian preschool children]. Unpublished raw data.

Federal Interagency Forum on Child and Family Statistics. *America's Children in Brief: Key National Indicators of Well-Being, 2010.* Washington, DC: U.S. Government Printing Office.

Frigerio, A., Cozzi, P., Pastore, V., Molteni, M., Borgatti, R., & Montirosso, R. (2006). The evaluation of behavioral and emotional problems in a sample of Italian preschoolers using the Child Behavior Checklist and the Caregiver-Teacher Report Form. *Infanzia e Adolescenza, 5,* 24-32.

Gerhardstein, R. R., Lonigan, C. J., Cukrowicz, K. C., & McGuffey, J. A. (2003). Factor structure of the Conners' Teacher Rating Scale-Short Form in a low-income preschool sample. *Journal of Psychoeducational Assessment, 21,* 223-243.

Gudmundsson, H., & Bjarnadottir, G. (2009). [Child Behavior Checklist/1½-5 and C-TRF scores for Icelandic preschool children]. Unpublished raw data.

Goodman, R. (1997). The Strengths and Difficulties Questionnaire: A research note. *Journal of Child Psychology and Psychiatry, 38,* 581-586.

Hu, L., & Bentler, P. (1999). Cutoff criteria for fit indexes in covariance structure analysis: Conventional criteria versus new alternatives. *Structural Equation Modeling, 6,* 1-55. doi: 10.1080/10705519909540118

Ivanova, M. Y., Achenbach, T. M., Dumenci, L., Rescorla, L. A., Almqvist, F., Bilenberg, N.,....Verhulst, F. C. (2007a). Testing the 8-syndrome structure of the Child Behavior Checklist in 30 societies. *Journal of Clinical Child and Adolescent Psychology, 36,* 405-417. doi: 10.1080/15374410701444363

Ivanova, M. Y., Achenbach, T. M., Rescorla, L. A., Dumenci, L., Almqvist, F., Bathiche, M.,....Verhulst, F. C. (2007b). Testing the generalizability of the Teacher's Report Form syndromes in 20 societies. *School Psychology Review, 36,* 468-483.

Ivanova, M. Y., Achenbach, T. M., Rescorla, L. A., Dumenci, L., Almqvist, F., Bilenberg, N.,....Verhulst, F. C. (2007c). The generalizability of the Youth Self-Report syndrome structure in 23 societies. *Journal of Consulting and Clinical Psychology, 75,* 729-738. doi: 10.1037/0022-0006X.75.5.729

Ivanova, M. Y., Achenbach, T. M., Rescorla, L. A., Harder, V. S., Ang, R. P., Bilenberg, N.,....Verhulst, F. C. (2010). Preschool psychopathology reported by parents in 23 societies: Testing the seven-syndrome model of the Child Behavior Checklist for Ages 1.5-5. *Journal of the American Academy of Child and Adolescent Psychiatry, 49,* 1215-1224.

Johnson, R., Gomez, F. C., & Sanders-Phillips, K. (1999). Factor structure and subtest differences on the Preschool Behavior Questionnaire in a Latino, African-American, Euro-American, and Asian preschool population. *Psychological Reports, 84,* 936-942.

Jusiene, R., Raiziene, S., Barkauskiene, R., Bielauskaite, R., & Dervinyte-Bongarzoni. A. (2007). The risk factors of emotional and behavioral problems in preschool age. *Visuomenes Ssveikata [Public Health], 4,* 46-54.

Koglen, U., Barquero, B., Mayer, H., Scheithauer, H., & Petermann, F. (2007). German version of the Strengths and Difficulties Questionnaire (T4-16 SDQ): Psychometric quality of the teacher version for preschoolers. *Diagnostica, 53,* 175-183.

Kristensen, S., Henriksen, T. B., & Bilenberg, N. (2010). The Child Behavior Checklist for Ages 1.5-5 (CBCL/1½-5): Assessment and analysis of parent- and caregiver-reported problems in a population-based sample of Danish preschool children. *Nordic Journal of Psychiatry, 64,* 203-209.

LaFreniere, P. J., & Dumas, J. E. (1996). Social competence and behavior evaluation in children ages 3 to 6 years: The short form (SCBE-30). *Psychological Assessment, 8,* 369-377.

LaFreniere, P., Masataka, N., Butovskaya, M., Chen, Q., Dessen, M. A., Atwanger, K., & Frigerio, A. (2002). Cross-cultural analysis of social competence and behavior problems in preschoolers. *Early Education and Development, 13,* 201-219.

Lecannelier, F., Lobel, S. P., Mas, P. O., Rodriguez, J. T., & Rojas, P. O. (2011) [C-TRF scores for Chilean preschool children]. Unpublished raw data.

Liu, J., Cheng, H., & Leung, P. W. L. (2010). The application of the preschool Child Behavior Checklist and Caregiver-Teacher Report Form to mainland Chinese children: Syndrome structure, gender differences, country effects, and inter-informant agreement. *Journal of Abnormal Child Psychology, 39,* 251-264.

Markovic, J. (2010). [Child Behavior Checklist/1½-5 and C-TRF scores for Serbian preschool children]. Unpublished raw data.

Marsh, H. W., Hau, K. T., & Wen, Z. (2004). In search of golden rules: Comment on hypothesis-testing approaches to setting cutoff values for fit indices and dangers in overgeneralizing Hu and Bentler's (1999) findings. *Structural Equation Modeling, 11,* 320-341.

Muratori, F., Narzisi, A., Igliozzi, R., Parrini, B., & Tancredi, R. (2008). La CBCL come strumento di screening per il Disturbo Pervasivo dello Sviluppo nei bambini prescolari. *Autismo e Disturbie Pervasivi Dello Sviluppo, 6,* 29-43.

McDonald, R. P. (2004). Respecifying improper structures. *Structural Equation Modeling, 11,*194-209.

Muthén, L. L., & Muthén, B. O. (2009). *Mplus: User's guide.* Los Angeles: Muthén & Muthén.

Rescorla, L. A., Achenbach, T. M., Ivanova, M. Y., Bilenberg, N., Bjarnadottir, G., Denner, S.,....Verhulst, F. C. Behavioral/emotional problems of preschoolers: Reports by caregivers/teachers in 15 societies. *Journal of Emotional and Behavioral Disorders.*

Rubin, K. H., Moller, L., & Emptage, A. (1987). The Preschool Behaviour Questionnaire: A useful index of behaviour problems in elementary school-age children? *Canadian Journal of Behavioural Science, 19,* 86-100. doi: 10.1037/h0079884

Schmeck, K., & Skrabel, C. (2004). [Child Behavior Checklist/1½-5 and C-TRF scores for Austrian preschool children]. Unpublished raw data.

Pronaj, A. A., & Shahini, M. (2010, April). *Emotional and behavioral problems in children 2-5 years old in Kosovo kindergartens, reported by teachers.* Presented at the national conference of the Albanian Psychiatric Association, Tirane, Albania.

Sikora, D. S., Hall, T. A., Hartley, S. L., Gerrard-Morris, A., & Cagle, S. (2008). Does parent report of behavior differ across ADOS-G classifications: Analysis of scores from the CBCL and GARS. *Journal of Autism and Developmental Disorders, 38*, 440-448.

Tick, N. T., van der Ende, J., Koot, H. M., & Verhulst, F. C. (2007). 14-year changes in emotional and behavioral problems of very young Dutch children. *Journal of the American Academy of Child and Adolescent Psychiatry, 46,* 1333-1340.

Tucker, L. R., & Lewis, C. (1973). The reliability coefficient for maximum likelihood factor analysis. *Psychometrika, 38*, 1-10.

Van Driel, O. P. (1978). On various causes of improper solutions in maximum likelihood factor analysis. *Psychometrika, 43,* 225-243.

Yu, C. Y., & Muthén, B. O. (2002). *Evaluation of model fit indices for latent variable models with categorical and continuous outcomes* (Technical Report). Los Angeles: UCLA, Graduate School of Education and Information Studies.

Internalizing and Externalizing Symptoms in Two-Year-Olds: Links to Mother-Toddler Emotion Processes

Sarah E. Martin
Simmons College

Mari L. Clements
Fuller Theological Seminary

Keith A. Crnic
Arizona State University

This study focused on mother-toddler emotion processes as related to internalizing and externalizing behavior problems in 2-year-old children. Participants were 59 toddlers (ages 24- to 35-months) and their mothers. Dyads were observed in two interactive contexts (Free Play and Waiting Task) and rated along global dimensions of responsiveness and emotion sharing. Mothers completed questionnaire measures of child behavior problems and maternal depressive symptoms. Findings suggested that parent-child emotion processes were associated with both internalizing and externalizing symptoms in 2-year-old children, although the nature of these associations varied across the interaction contexts in which these processes were assessed. With respect to the Free Play interaction, children's emotional responsiveness to their mothers was associated with internalizing behavior symptoms, with less responsive children evidencing more mother-reported internalizing problems. During the Waiting Task, children's emotional responsiveness and shared negative emotion were associated with child externalizing behavior symptoms, with less responsiveness and more shared negativity associated with increased externalizing symptoms. Maternal depression made modest contributions to both internalizing and externalizing symptoms. Findings suggest that the study of parent-child emotion processes may contribute to our understanding of internalizing and externalizing behavior problems as expressed in toddlers, with implications for early assessment and intervention.

Keywords: mother-child interaction, internalizing and externalizing problems, emotions, toddlers

Correspondence concerning this article should be addressed to: Sarah Martin, Department of Psychology, Simmons College, 300 The Fenway, Boston, MA 02115. E-mail: sarah.martin@simmons.edu

The developmental processes associated with emotion and emotion regula-
tion are fundamental to early mental health and psychopathology (Cole & Deater-
Deckard, 2009; Izard, Youngstrom, Fine, Mostow, & Trentacosta, 2006). Indeed,
early difficulties in the experience, expression, and management of emotion appear
central to the emergence and maintenance of child behavior disorders (e.g., Cole,
Michel, & Teti, 1994; Frick & Morris, 2004; Shaw, Keenan, Vondra, Delliquadri,
& Giovannelli, 1997; Silk, Shaw, Forbes, Lane, & Kovacs, 2006; Zeman, Shipman,
& Suveg, 2002). Further, for very young children, such affective processes occur
in the context of their social environment and unfold in the course of their dyadic
interactions with caregivers. As such, a focus on parent-child emotion processes
may offer important insight into the nature and interactive contexts of behavior
problems as expressed in early childhood.

Mother-Toddler Emotions and Child Behavior Problems

There has been increasing theoretical and empirical attention devoted to the
nature and function of emotions within early dyadic interactions. Constructs
such as synchrony (Harrist & Waugh, 2002; Skuban, Shaw, Garnder, Supplee, &
Nichols, 2006), mutuality (Deater-Deckard & Petrill, 2004; Lindsey, Cremeens, &
Caldera, 2010), interactive contingency (Beebe et al., 2008), mutual responsiveness
(Kochanska, 1997), emotional availability (Biringen, 2000), and co-regulation or
mutual regulation (Fogel, 1993; Tronick, 1989) have been introduced to describe
the dyadic and co-created nature of emotion within social interaction. Despite
the varying terms used to describe these interactive processes, such constructs
are similarly focused on the bi-directional and co-constructed nature of emotions
within parent-child interaction. In addition, most conceptualizations include attention to dimensions of *responsiveness* (i.e., the extent to which parent and child
engage in reciprocal and contingent emotional and behavioral exchanges) and
emotion sharing (i.e., the extent to which affective states are simultaneously experienced). More specifically, there is evidence to suggest that parents and young
children jointly influence the emotional course of their interactions by adjusting
their emotion and behavior in concert with the signals of their interaction partner
(i.e., responsiveness), such that the sharing of positive states (i.e., positive emotion sharing) is promoted and the sharing of negative states (i.e., negative emotion
sharing) is minimized (e.g., Cole, Teti, & Zahn-Waxler, 2003; Lindsey, Cremeens,
Colwell, & Caldera, 2009).

Research has suggested that parent-child emotion processes are associated
with a variety of child developmental competencies, including self-regulation,
compliance, communication skills, and social interactions with peers (Harrist,
Petit, Dodge, & Bates, 1994; Lehman, Steier, Guidash, & Wanna, 2002; Lindsey
et al., 2010; Lindsey et al., 2009; Raver, 1996; Rocissano, Slade, & Lynch, 1987).
Moreover, there is growing empirical evidence to suggest that difficulties in the

dyadic regulation of emotion may be associated with early childhood behavior problems. Specifically, parent-child interactions characterized by lower levels of contingent responding, less shared positive emotion, and heightened levels of shared negative emotion have been associated with increased child externalizing behavior problems, including disruptive behavior symptoms, aggressiveness, and noncompliance (Cole et al., 2003; Criss, Shaw, & Ingoldsby, 2003; Deater-Deckard, Atzaba-Poria, & Pike, 2004; Deater-Deckard & Petrill, 2004). Several studies have also suggested that there may be gender-specific associations between parent-child emotion processes and children's behavioral adjustment (e.g., Cole et al., 2003; Lindsey et al., 2009), with evidence to suggest that young boys may be particularly affected by the emotional dynamics of parent-child interaction and more susceptible to poor outcomes in the context of non-optimal interaction patterns. Interestingly, parent-child emotion processes have been infrequently examined in relation to early internalizing behavior problems (e.g., depressive or anxiety symptoms), despite compelling theoretical arguments for the role of emotions in the development of such problems (Cole, Luby, & Sullivan, 2008).

The toddlerhood years represent an important period in which to examine parent-child emotion processes as linked to both internalizing and externalizing behavior problems. This developmental period has been characterized as emotionally challenging for both children and their caregivers and as presenting related risks for early maladaptation (e.g., Belsky, Woodward, & Crnic, 1996; Keenan & Wakschlag, 2000). These developmental challenges provide opportunities for growth and consolidation of toddlers' emerging emotion regulation skills, or alternatively, may tax and overwhelm a dyad's capacities for synchronous interaction, resulting in increased risk for associated problems in child adjustment. A focus on the toddlerhood years is also consistent with the field's growing awareness that emotional and behavioral difficulties occur in early childhood (e.g., Zeanah, 2009) and with evidence suggesting that, for many young children, such difficulties are not merely transient phases, but rather early indicators of more persistent mental health problems (e.g., Briggs-Gowan, Carter, Bosson-Hennan, Guver, & Horwitz, 2006). This is also a developmental period during which early internalizing and externalizing difficulties may become increasingly distinct from normative variation in toddler aggressiveness, uncooperative behavior, and emotional dyscontrol (e.g., Carter, Godoy, Wagmiller, Marakovitz, & Briggs-Gowen, 2010; Luby, 2009; Wakschlag & Danis, 2009). As such, a focus on 2-year-olds may offer important insight into the early expression of externalizing and internalizing behavior problems, particularly as related to dyadic emotion and interactive behaviors.

Emotions in Context: Role of Maternal Depression and
Interactive Conditions

It is also important to identify contextual factors that may contribute to variability in the emotional qualities of parent-child interaction and associated difficulties in adjustment. In this regard, a focus on maternal depression may be particularly informative. Mothers of young children are at increased risk for experiencing depressive symptoms and disorder (Lyons-Ruth, Wolfe, Lyubchik, & Steingard, 2002) and maternal distress and depression have been consistently identified as risk factors for disturbances in the dyadic regulation of parent-child emotion, including disruptions in responsiveness and emotion sharing (Beebe et al., 2008; Dix & Meunier, 2009; Reck et al., 2004; Tronick, 1989). For example, during interactions with their toddlers, depressed mothers have been found to demonstrate less interactive coordination, decreased engagement, more conflict, and less positivity (Caughy, Huang, & Lima, 2009; Feng, Shaw, Skuban, & Lane, 2007; Jameson, Gelfand, Kulscar, & Teti, 1997). Caregiver depression has been similarly implicated in the development of child behavior problems, including both internalizing and externalizing difficulties (Downey & Coyne, 1990; Elgar, McGrath, Waschbusch, Stewart, & Curtis, 2004; Silk et al., 2006), with even non-clinical levels of parental emotional upset linked to problematic child outcomes (Gartstein & Bateman, 2008; West & Newman, 2003).

A focus on parent-child emotion may contribute to our understanding of the links between maternal depression and toddler internalizing and externalizing behavior problems. For example, to the extent that depressive symptoms interfere with maternal responsiveness and emotion sharing, disrupted parent-child emotion processes may be a mechanism by which maternal depression is linked to toddler adjustment problems. Evidence for this possibility comes from several recent studies. For example, the NICHD Early Child Care Research Network (2004) found that affective dysregulation at 24 months (as indexed by children's expressions of negativity and defiance within mother-child interaction) was associated with maternal depression and predictive of children's less competent social functioning and increased child externalizing symptoms, but not internalizing symptoms, at 36 months. More recently, Leckman-Westin, Cohen, and Stueve (2009) examined maternal depressive symptoms and quality of mother-toddler interaction (including affective tone and maternal responsivity) as associated with children's concurrent problem behaviors (i.e., tantrums, crying, fearfulness) and behavioral adjustment at school age. Their findings suggested that both increased maternal depressive symptoms and non-optimal dyadic interaction patterns were associated with higher levels of mother-reported toddler behavior problems. Lower maternal responsivity was also associated with problem behaviors in toddlerhood and moderated the associations between maternal depressive symptoms and later child outcomes. These studies support the value of examining the links between maternal depressive symptoms, parent-child emotions, and toddler behavior problems, and of evaluating the specific problem behaviors and symptom profiles that may be related to both maternal depression and associated dyadic interaction patterns.

Finally, the study of emotions in early parent-child interaction must also consider the situational contexts in which these interactions unfold. Contemporary theories of emotion stress the functional nature of emotions which serve to prepare the individual to interact with his or her environment; as such, emotions and social interactions occur within context and in relation to situational demands. For young children and their caregivers, dyadic regulation may proceed quite differently depending on the environments in which it occurs, the goals of the interaction, and the resources available to facilitate effective emotion management (Dennis, Cole, Wiggins, Cohen, & Zalewski, 2009). For example, cross-situational differences have been identified in the emotions and regulatory strategies of 2-year-olds (e.g., Grolnick, Bridges, & Connell, 1996) and 3-year-olds (Dennis et al.; Stansbury & Sigman, 2000; Zimmerman & Stansbury, 2003), as well as in the emotionally interactive behaviors displayed by their caregivers (Smith, Calkins, & Keane, 2006). It is also possible that the links between maternal depressive symptoms, parent-toddler emotions, and children's behavioral adjustment may be more evident in some contexts than in others (e.g., contexts that are more inherently taxing and require higher levels of maternal engagement and emotional responsiveness; Birigen et al., 2005; Rodriguez et al., 2005).

To date, few studies have specifically examined the role of context as shaping parent-toddler interactive behaviors or in influencing the associations with parent or child outcomes, more often assessing parent-child dyads within a single interactive context (e.g., Lindsey, Mize, & Petit, 1997) or combining ratings of interactive behavior assessed in multiple contexts (e.g., Skuban et al., 2006). Of notable exception is a recent study by Lindsey and colleagues (2010), focusing on parent-toddler mutuality (i.e., defined as parent and child responsiveness to initiations and shared positive emotion) as linked to children's peer relationship functioning. Indeed, Lindsey and colleagues found that greater mother-toddler mutuality during play was associated with children's more prosocial behavior with peers, whereas greater mutuality during a caregiving activity was associated with lower aggressiveness with peers. Although they did not focus on internalizing and externalizing behavior symptoms per se, their findings are relevant insofar as the quality of toddlers' peer interactions may be linked to other manifestations of their behavioral adjustment. For example, lower levels of prosocial behavior may reflect withdrawal or less positive engagement with others (i.e., consistent with emergent internalizing behavior problems) whereas higher levels of peer aggressiveness may suggest difficulties with frustration tolerance, impulse control, and compliance with behavioral expectations (i.e., consistent with emergent externalizing problems). These findings point to the need to examine dyadic interaction across tasks that involve different emotional demands and goals, and to examine context-specific emotion processes as related to child behavioral adjustment.

Summary and Goals of the Study

Taken together, the available literature supports the value of examining parent-child emotion processes as related to behavior problems during toddlerhood; however, an understanding of the associations to expressions of toddler maladjustment (i.e., internalizing vs. externalizing symptoms) is only beginning to emerge. In addition, there has been limited attention to the links between maternal depressive symptoms, mother-toddler emotions, and toddler behavior problems or to the role of interactive context as influencing these associations. As such, the goals of this study were:

1. to describe mother-toddler emotion processes (including dimensions of parent-child responsiveness and emotion sharing, observed in two different interactive contexts) in a sample of 2-year-olds and their mothers,
2. to examine the associations between mother-toddler emotion processes and toddlers' internalizing and externalizing behavior problems and to explore the role of gender as influencing these associations, and
3. to examine multivariate associations between mother-toddler emotion processes, maternal depressive symptoms, and toddler's behavior problem symptoms.

Method

Participants

Participants were 60 toddlers and their mothers who were participating in a larger study of parent-child interaction and early emotional development (Martin, Clements, & Crnic, 2002). One mother-toddler dyad was eliminated from analyses (due to missing child behavior problem data), resulting in a sample of 59 children (25 girls, 34 boys) and their mothers. All children were 2 years old at the time of their participation (range = 24.1 to 35.9 months, $M = 30.1$ months, $SD = 3.8$ months). Participating families were living in a semi-rural area of the northeast and were recruited through newspaper advertisements, newspaper birth announcements, and fliers placed at community locations. Reflecting the surrounding community, the majority of participants (93%) were European American. Most participating mothers (90%) were married at the time of the laboratory visit. Mothers reported a mean age of 33.9 years ($SD = 4.6$ years). Mothers had, on average, completed 4 years of post-high school education.

Procedures

Mothers and toddlers participated in a laboratory session as part of a larger study on parent-child interaction and early emotional development. Only the tasks and measures relevant to the current study will be described here[1]. Mothers completed self-report measures of depressive symptoms and child behavior problems. Following completion of self-report measures, mother-toddler dyads participated in several structured and unstructured interactions in the laboratory; these interactions were videotaped for later observational coding. Dyads first participated in a 7-minute, unstructured Free Play time, with attractive, age-appropriate toys available (e.g., dolls, trains, blocks). This task was intended to be mutually enjoyable for mothers and toddlers, and was expected to elicit mostly positive and pleasant parent-child interaction. In addition, dyads participated in a 5-minute Waiting Task (Carmichael-Olson, Greenberg, & Slough, 1985). During this procedure, children were presented with an attractively wrapped gift, but instructed to wait to open the gift until their mother had completed several additional questionnaires. This procedure was intended to be emotionally taxing for both toddlers and mothers, as children were required to delay gratification and inhibit behavior, and mothers were faced with potentially competing tasks (i.e., completing questionnaires and managing child behavior). In addition to the child's gift, families were paid $15 for their participation in the study.

Measures

Maternal depression. Maternal depression was assessed using the *Center for Epidemiological Studies Depression Scale* (CES-D; Radloff, 1977). The CES-D is a 20-item self-report measure of depressive symptoms. Mothers reported on the frequency with which they experienced a variety of depressive symptoms (e.g., irritability, sleep and appetite disturbance, crying, feelings of sadness and depression) during the past two weeks, using a scale from 1 (rarely or none of the time, less than 1 day) to 4 (most or all of the time, 5 – 7 days). Items were summed to create a total symptom severity score; a score of 16 has been validated as a clinical cutoff, differentiating depressed and nondepressed adults in both clinical and nonclinical samples. The CES-D has been shown to have good reliability and to be valid for use in community samples (e.g., Santor, Zuroff, Ramsay, Cervantes, & Palacios, 1995), with good internal consistency in the current sample, $\alpha = .86$.

---

[1] In addition to the measures and tasks described for the current study, dyads participated in a story-telling activity and a toy clean-up task. Mothers also completed several additional questionnaires focusing on family emotionality, parenting, marital functioning, and child behavior.

Child behavior problems. Child behavior problems were assessed using the *Child Behavior Checklist for 2 -3 Year Olds* (CBCL/2-3; Achenbach, Edelbrock, & Howell, 1987). The CBCL/2-3 is a 94-item checklist, which yields broad band scales of Internalizing and Externalizing behavior problems. Mothers reported on the extent to which their child demonstrated specific emotional and behavioral problems, from 0 (not at all true of my child) to 2 (very true of my child), and scores are summed across items on the scales. The CBCL/2-3 has been shown to have good test-retest reliability (mean r for scales = .87), and to be predictive of parent-reported behavior problems up to 3 years later (Achenbach et al.). In clinical settings, the CBCL/2-3 is scored to provide T scores to facilitate identification of clinically elevated scores. Due to the nonclinical nature of the current sample, raw scores rather than T scores were analyzed.

Observational coding of mother-toddler emotion processes. Mother-toddler emotion processes were assessed during the Free Play and Waiting Task, using an observational coding system developed for this study. The coding system was derived from an existing system for assessing parent-child and family interaction (Belsky, Hsieh, & Crnic, 1998), with a specific focus on the emotional qualities of mother-toddler interaction. Specifically, global ratings were used to characterize each dyad's degree of responsiveness and emotion sharing during each of the two interaction tasks (Free Play and Waiting Task).

For each interaction task, dyads were rated along four dimensions, each using a Likert-type scale (1 = *minimal/absent* to 5 = *high*): (a) Mother Responsiveness (i.e., the extent to which the mother demonstrated emotional engagement and sensitivity/responsiveness to the child's emotion cues), (b) Child Responsiveness (i.e., the extent to which the child demonstrated emotional engagement and responsiveness to mother's affective and interactive bids), (c) Shared Positive Emotion (i.e., the extent to which members of dyad simultaneously expressed positive emotions such as joy or interest), and (d) Shared Negative Emotion (i.e., the extent to which members of the dyad simultaneously expressed negative emotions such as frustration, irritation, or distress). The codes used to assess these dimensions are described inTable 1; the full coding system is available from the first author.

All coding was completed by two independent undergraduate coders who were trained and supervised by the first author. Both coders reached a criterion of r_{ICC} = .70 on demonstration tapes prior to beginning coding. Coders were uninformed of the hypotheses of the study and unaware of participants' responses on measures of maternal depression or child behavior problems. Twelve (20%) of the videotapes of mother-toddler interaction were independently coded by both coders and inter-rater reliability was assessed using intraclass correlations. As shown in Table 1, inter-rater reliability ranged from acceptable to high, mean r_{ICC} = .86. Not surprisingly, given the demands of the tasks, there was greater variability–and thus greater reliability–in mother and toddler behavior in the Waiting task than in the Free Play task, as shown in Table 2. This was most notable with Shared Negative

Table 1

Description of observational coding and inter-rater reliability (r_{ICC}) for mother-toddler emotion processes

Code	Description	r_{ICC} Free Play	r_{ICC} Waiting Task
Mother Responsiveness	This code reflects the extent to which the mother is "tuned in" to the emotional experiences and needs of her child. A mother rated as high on responsiveness appears aware of her child's moods and emotional needs and allows this awareness to guide her interactions with the child. Highly responsive mothers may engage in behaviors that include emotion labeling, emotion matching (i.e., adjusting her emotions to match those of the child), sensitive and appropriate responding to the child's displays of emotion, and encouraging the child's positive emotion states.	.68	.68
Child Responsiveness	This code reflects the extent to which the child appears "tuned in" or emotionally connected to the mother; includes the extent to which the child responds to the mother when she attempts to engage or soothe them, as well as the child's responsiveness to the mother's bids and suggestions. Highly responsive children appear emotionally engaged and respond quickly and readily to the mother. Unresponsive children may appear resistant or avoidant with respect to their mother's attempts to influence their emotion states.	.74	.95
Shared Positive Emotion	This code reflects the extent to which positive emotion is shared (i.e., simultaneously experienced) by both members of the dyad; positive emotion is evidenced by facial expressions, vocalizations, or behavioral indicators of happiness, amusement, relaxation, and comfort. Dyads high on this code frequently demonstrate shared positive emotion, enthusiasm, and mutual enjoyment.	.75	.94
Shared Negative Emotion	This code reflects the extent to which conflict and negative emotion is shared (i.e., simultaneously experienced) by both members of the dyad. Dyads high on this code demonstrate high levels of shared negative emotion, as evidenced by observed conflict, tension, and/or vented hostility between members of the dyad.	--	.97

Table 2

Means, Standard Deviations, and Bivariate Correlations for Mother-Toddler Emotion Processes, Child Behavior Problems, and Maternal Depression

	M	SD	1.	2.	3.	4.	5.	6.	7.	8.	9.	10.
Mother-Toddler Emotion: Free Play												
1. Mother Responsive	4.31	0.70	--									
2. Child Responsive	4.25	0.71	.47**	--								
3. Shared Positive Emotion	2.88	0.62	.24^a	.19	--							
Mother-Toddler Emotion: Waiting Task												
4. Mother Responsive	4.22	0.83	.40**	.12	.29*	--						
5. Child Responsive	4.03	1.00	.18	.25*	.14	.39**	--					
6. Shared Positive Emotion	2.31	0.90	.23^a	.07	.35**	.51**	.39*	--				
7. Shared Negative Emotion§	1.15	0.52	-.28*	-.08	-.26^a	-.43**	-.42**	-.44**	--			
Child Behavior Problems												
8. CBCL Internalizing	7.07	3.74	.02	-.32*	-.17	.05	-.03	.09	-.01	--		
9. CBCL Externalizing	12.49	5.91	.06	-.13	-.11	-.01	-.30*	-.07	.25^a	.57**	--	
Maternal Depression												
10. CES-D	8.87	6.69	-.12	-.17	-.22a	-.02	-.04	.01	.09	.30*	.26*	--

Note. CBCL = Child Behavior Checklist; CES-D = Center for Epidemiological Studies Depression Scale. Pearson correlations (r) were used for all analyses except those including Shared Negative Emotion, for which Spearman's rho (^{rs}) was used.

*p < .05. **p < .01. ^{a}p < .10.

Emotion, which was essentially absent from the Free Play task, so Free Play Shared Negative Emotion was dropped from all analyses.

Results

Mother-Toddler Emotion Processes: Descriptive Analyses

Means and standard deviations for study variables are presented in Table 2. As shown, observational ratings suggested high levels of mother and child responsiveness, moderately high levels of shared positive emotion, and low levels of shared negative emotion[1]. Consistent with the nonclinical nature of this sample, mean scores for maternal depression and child behavior problems were well within the average range: only 8 mothers (13.6%) had CES-D scores above the established clinical cutoff (total score > 16) and 8 children were reported to be functioning above the borderline clinical range on one or both broadband CBCL scales.

The data were examined for possible gender differences in any of the study variables. A series of t-tests revealed no gender differences in child internalizing problems, maternal depression, or any observational ratings of parent-child emotion during either the Free Play or Waiting Task (all $ts < 1.47$, all $ps > .10$). Boys ($M = 14.38, SD = 5.79$) were reported to demonstrate more externalizing problems than girls ($M = 9.92, SD = 5.12$), $t (57) = 3.07, p < .01$.

Bivariate Associations Between Mother-Toddler Emotion and Child Behavior Problems

A set of correlations were computed to examine bivariate associations between study variables, including associations between mother-toddler emotion processes and toddler behavior problems (Table 2). With respect to observational ratings of mother-toddler interaction during Free Play, children rated as lower in responsiveness during play were reported to have more internalizing symptoms. Within the

---

[1] Most study variables were normally distributed, with the following exceptions: within the Waiting Task, ratings of Mother Responsiveness, Child Responsiveness, and Shared Negative Emotion were skewed (skew = -1.37, $z = 4.30, p < .001$; -1.14, $z = -3.57, p < .001$; and 4.04, $z = 12.67, p < .001$, respectively). As recommended by Leech, Barrett, and Morgan (2008), the Mother and Child Responsiveness variables were transformed by squaring and skewness values for the resulting variables fell within recommended guidelines (skew = 0.54 and 0.55, respectively. These transformed variables were used in all subsequent analyses, although for ease of interpretation, the means and standard deviations presented in Table 2 reflect the untransformed variables. Standard transformation procedures were applied to the Shared Negative Emotion variable, but these did not effectively correct the observed skewness. Therefore, nonparametric statistics were used when appropriate for analyses that included this variable.

Waiting Task, children rated as less responsive were reported to have more externalizing symptoms. In addition, the association between shared negative emotion during the wait and toddlers' externalizing symptoms approached significance, with higher levels of shared negative emotion associated with more symptoms.

A second set of correlations were computed to explore possible gender differences in the pattern of bivariate associations between mother-toddler emotion processes and child behavior problems; these analyses are not tabled here but are available from the first author. Analyses revealed that the overall pattern of associations between mother-toddler emotion and child behavior problems was quite similar for boys and girls, with two exceptions. The association between children's responsiveness during Free Play and internalizing behavior problems was significant for boys ($r = -.41, p = .02$) but not girls ($r = -.19, p = .36$), although these correlations were not significantly different via Fisher's z-test. In addition, the association between shared negative emotion during the Waiting Task and externalizing behavior problems approached significance for boys ($r_s = .32, p = .06$) but not for girls ($r_s = -.11, p = .59$) and this difference also approached significance via z-test ($p = .06$). Given the overall gender difference in levels of externalizing problems and these possible differences in patterns of associations, gender was retained as a variable in all subsequent multivariate analyses.

Multivariate Associations between Child Gender, Maternal Depression, Mother-Toddler Emotion, and Child Behavior Problems

Two hierarchical multiple regression analyses were conducted to examine the relative contributions of child gender, maternal depressive symptoms, and mother-toddler emotion processes in the statistical prediction of toddler internalizing and externalizing symptoms, respectively. Given gender differences in children's externalizing symptom severity and in the bivariate associations between some mother-toddler emotion processes and child symptoms, gender was entered at the first step in each regression. Because previous research has clearly demonstrated the importance of maternal depression as related to children's behavior problems (e.g., Downey & Coyne, 1990; Elgar et al., 2004; Feng et al., 2007), this variable was entered at the second step. Mother-toddler emotion variables were entered at the third step; in order to reduce the number of variables used in these analyses, only emotion variables demonstrating bivariate associations with the dependent variables with $p < .10$ were included in regression analyses. These regression analyses therefore allowed for examination of the unique contribution of mother-toddler emotion in the statistical prediction of child behavior problems, over and above the contributions of both gender and maternal depression. Assumptions for regression were checked and met for both analyses; the relationships between predictor and dependent variables were linear and residuals were normally distributed and uncorrelated with predictor variables.

Toddler internalizing symptoms. In the regression equation for child internalizing symptoms, predictor variables were child gender (Step 1), maternal depression (Step 2), and one mother-toddler emotion variable (Child Responsiveness during Free Play; Step 3). Child gender was not associated with toddler internalizing symptoms, $R^2 = .04$, $F = 2.17$, $p = .15$. However maternal depressive symptoms contributed significant variance at the second step, $\Delta R^2 = .08$, $\Delta F = 5.14$, $p = .03$, with increased maternal depression associated with more toddler internalizing symptoms. Inclusion of the mother-toddler emotion variable contributed additional variance at the third step, $\Delta R^2 = .08$, $\Delta F = 5.26$, $p = .03$, with less responsive children demonstrating more internalizing symptoms. The final regression equation was significant, $R^2 = .20$, $F (3, 55) = 4.43$, $p < .01$, with lower child responsiveness and increased maternal depression associated with more toddler internalizing symptoms (Table 3).

Toddler externalizing symptoms. Child gender (Step 1) and maternal depression (Step 2) were included as predictor variables in the regression analyses for child externalizing symptoms. In addition, two mother-toddler emotion variables (Child Responsiveness and Shared Negative Emotion during the Waiting Task) were associated with children's externalizing symptoms and were therefore to be included in the regression analysis. However, the significant association between these variables ($r_s = -.42$, $p < .01$) suggested that multicollinearity was of concern. A composite variable was therefore computed by summing observational ratings of Shared Negative Emotion (reverse scored) and Child Responsiveness. The resulting composite variable was slightly skewed (skew = -1.87) and corrected by cubing (skew = -0.94).

Regression analysis indicated that male gender was associated with more externalizing behavior problems, $R^2 = .14$, $F (1, 57) = 9.42$, $p < .01$. The prediction was modestly but not significantly improved by the inclusion of maternal depressive symptoms at the second step, $\Delta R^2 = .05$, $\Delta F = 3.42$, $p = .07$. Inclusion of the composite mother-toddler emotion variable (Waiting Task Child Responsiveness/ Shared Negative Emotion) made a significant contribution at the third step, $\Delta R^2 = .09$, $\Delta F = 6.72$, $p = .01$, with less optimal parent-toddler interaction (i.e., lower child responsiveness and more shared negative emotion) associated with more externalizing symptoms. The final regression equation was significant, $R^2 = .28$, $F (3, 55) = 7.10$, $p < .001$, with both gender and mother-toddler emotion processes contributing significant variance. Maternal depressive symptoms made a trend-level contribution to the final prediction (Table 3).

Discussion

Findings of the present study contribute to an understanding of the developmental significance of parent-child emotion processes during toddlerhood, particularly as related to early problem behaviors. In keeping with recent theoretical

Table 3

Prediction of Toddler Internalizing and Externalizing Behavior Problems by Gender, Maternal Depression, and Mother-Toddler Emotion Processes

Predictor	CBCL Internalizing Problems			CBCL Externalizing Problems		
	B	SE_B	β	B	SE_B	β
Step 1						
Gender	1.43	0.98	.19	4.46	1.45	.38**
Step 2						
Gender	1.23	0.95	.16	4.21	1.43	.36**
CES-D	0.16	0.07	.29*	0.20	0.11	.22[a]
Step 3						
Gender	1.30	0.91	.17	3.70	1.38	.31*
CES-D	0.13	0.07	.24[a]	0.19	0.10	.21[a]
Mother-Toddler Emotion Processes						
Child Responsiveness (Free Play)	-1.49	0.65	-.28*	--	--	--
Child Responsiveness/Shared Negative Emotion (Waiting Task)	--	--	--	-0.01	0.001	-.30*

Note. CBCL = Child Behavior Checklist; CES-D = Center for Epidemiological Studies Depression Scale

*$p < .05$. **$p < .01$. [a]$p < .10$.

and empirical work in this area (e.g., Harrist & Waugh, 2002; Lindsey et al., 2008; Skuban et al., 2006), we focused particularly on the inter-related dimensions of parent-child responsiveness and emotion sharing and predicted associations to toddler internalizing and externalizing behavior symptoms. We also examined the multivariate associations between mother-toddler emotion processes, toddler behavior problems, maternal depressive symptoms, and child gender. Indeed, findings suggested that mother-toddler emotion processes were associated with both internalizing and externalizing symptoms in 2-year-old children, although the nature of these associations varied across the contexts in which mother-toddler interaction was observed. Specifically, internalizing symptoms were linked to children's responsiveness during the relatively unstructured and positive task of Free Play, whereas externalizing symptoms were associated with child responsiveness and shared negative emotion during the more taxing Waiting Task.

Mother-Toddler Emotion During Play: Links to Child Internalizing Behavior

With respect to toddler internalizing symptoms, children's responsiveness to their mothers (as observed during an unstructured Free Play interaction) was associated with internalizing symptoms, with less responsive children evidencing more mother-reported symptoms. More specifically, toddlers who were observed to be less emotionally engaged and receptive during dyadic play demonstrated more mother-reported internalizing symptoms. Such findings may reflect something of the nature of internalizing behaviors as expressed in very young children. Although toddlers and young preschoolers show emergent skills for emotional self-regulation, this developmental period is also characterized by children's continued reliance on caregiver-guided regulation strategies (Sroufe, 1996). As such, emotional competence during toddlerhood necessarily involves children's emotional connectedness to caregivers and openness to the regulatory support provided within these relationships. Toddlers' decreased responsiveness during parent-child play interactions may suggest emergent difficulties participating in the dyadic regulation of positive emotion states, such as joy or interest.

Such a possibility is also consistent with the finding that the association between toddler's responsiveness and internalizing behaviors emerged during Free Play and not during the Waiting Task interaction. The unstructured play context afford parents and children the opportunity to interact around a common goal (i.e., to facilitate child exploration and dyadic enjoyment) and to initiate and modulate positive emotion states. When young children participate effectively in these interactions, both parents and children may experience a sense of enjoyment, enthusiasm, and interpersonal connection. Over time, these experiences may contribute to children's sense of mastery with respect to regulation of their own and others' positive emotion experiences, a uniquely powerful tool for negotiating the emotional aspects of social interaction. In contrast, when dyads are unable to establish positive emotional responsiveness within their interactions, children may become less likely to anticipate positive and effective emotional exchanges within the family and other social interactions. In this way, young children's decreased emotional responsiveness during play interactions may reflect a more generalized difficulty in generating and reciprocating positive emotions within social interaction, problems that may be core to the development of internalizing behavior symptoms such as withdrawal, irritability, and lack of positive engagement.

Mother-Toddler Emotion During a Challenge: Links to Toddler Externalizing Behavior

A different set of interaction variables emerged as associated with toddler externalizing symptoms. Specifically, decreased child responsiveness and more shared negative emotion (as observed during the Waiting Task) were associated with more mother-reported externalizing symptoms. These findings contribute to a growing literature on parent-child emotion processes as linked to the development and expression of disruptive behavior problems in young children. Specifically, early emotional and behavioral dysregulation may be viewed in relational context and, arguably, as laying the affective groundwork for emergence of the mutually coercive interaction patterns associated with more enduring childhood disruptive behavior problems (Scaramella & Leve, 2004). Over time, toddlers and their mothers may rely on increasingly aversive strategies to engage their interaction partners and to regulate shared negative emotion states within their interactions. Consistent with functionalist perspectives on emotion regulation and developmental psychopathology (e.g., Cole et al., 1994; Cole, Dennis, Martin, & Hall, 2008), toddlers' disruptive behavior symptoms may serve adaptive short-term functions within their close relationships. For example, children may engage in aggressive or noncompliant behaviors in an effort to control or terminate an emotionally unpleasant interaction. Of course, over time, these "regulatory" efforts are likely to increase negative parent-child emotionality and may eventually coalesce into more stable patterns of behavioral disruption. Such difficulties may be particularly exacerbated when co-occurring with other child or family risk factors (e.g., difficult child temperament, heightened family stress).

Findings are also notable, although perhaps not surprising, in that the dyadic processes associated with toddler externalizing symptoms were observed under challenging interaction conditions (i.e., the Waiting Task), when children and mothers were faced with competing agendas and potential conflict. That is, in this task, the dyad was faced with the task of managing the negative affect associated with the competing goals of the child (e.g., anticipation of gift opening) and parent (e.g., prevention of the gift opening while completing an unrelated task). When caregivers and young children are unable to reconcile these competing goals, shared negative emotions may be generated and difficulties in dyadic regulation may emerge

In turn, these difficulties may well give rise to toddler externalizing problems. Findings also add to a growing literature suggesting that some facets of dyadic emotion may be most effectively assessed within stress contexts (e.g., Biringen et al., 2005). Although these dyadic patterns may eventually generalize to play or similarly low-stress interaction contexts, their earliest manifestations seem to be most evident when conflict potential and emotional stakes are high.

Findings were also consistent with literature to suggest that male children appear to be at increased risk for early externalizing behavior difficulties. Specifically, findings suggested that male gender was associated with more toddler externalizing symptoms and that the associations between mother-toddler shared negative emotion and externalizing symptoms was somewhat stronger for boys than for girls. Such findings may point to the emergence of gender-specific pathways to disruptive behavioral difficulties, with boys demonstrating somewhat greater susceptibility to the negative effects of emotionally asynchronous early parent-child interactions. Similar associational findings have also been interpreted as being due to greater variability in young boys' emotional and behavioral self-regulation (Lindsey et al., 2008). Of course, it was also the case that the gender differences identified in this study were few in number and small in magnitude, suggesting the need for cautious interpretation and additional research.

Finally, findings from multivariate analyses revealed that mother-toddler emotion processes were associated with toddler internalizing and externalizing behaviors, even after accounting for the influence of mothers' self-reported depressive symptoms, which also contributed modest but unique variance. Thus findings of the present study are consistent with the literature documenting significant associations between maternal depressive symptoms and early emerging child behavior problems and suggesting that such associations exist even when maternal symptoms may be relatively mild or "non-clinical" in severity (Gartstein & Bateman, 2008; West & Newman, 2003).

Limitations and Future Directions

Although findings of the present study contribute to our understanding of the role of mother-toddler emotion in the expression of behavioral symptoms in 2-year-old children, several limitations are of note. First, this study focused on a relatively small and homogeneous community sample of mothers and toddlers who evidenced low levels of child behavior problems and, consistent with other non-clinical samples (e.g., Leckman-Westin et al., 2009), relatively positive, responsive, and low-conflict interactive behaviors. As such, findings may not generalize to children at highest risk for early and enduring behavior problems, for example, children of families coping with more demographic or family stressors.

Relatedly, most mothers reported relatively low levels of depressive symptoms and it is certainly possible that findings may not extend to toddlers of mothers experiencing more severe symptoms or diagnosed disorder, or that the pattern of associations between mother-toddler emotions and child outcomes may differ in higher risk dyads. Further, although the CES-D is well-validated and widely used in developmental research, there is debate as to how to best interpret low scores on this and similar self-report scales (e.g., as the absence of depression, the denial of distress, or the presence of emotional well-being and happiness; Beebe et al., 2007; Pickens & Field, 1993; Tronick, Beeghly, Weinberg, & Olson, 1997; Wood, Taylor, & Joseph, 2010), as well as interest in nonlinear approaches to the analysis of self-reported maternal depression data (e.g., Beebe et al., 2008)[3]. As such, future work on mother-toddler emotion processes would be strengthened by inclusion of multiple measures of maternal depression, as well as more nuanced attention to issues of clinical thresholds and related relationship impairments.

In addition, future studies should incorporate additional measures of parent-toddler emotion processes. The coding of mother-toddler interaction was completed with an adaptation of an existing coding system, and replication of these findings in other samples will be important. In addition, the observational coding system used included only global ratings of parent-toddler interactive behavior. Although global ratings have been found to capture important, qualitative aspects of parent-child interaction (Bakeman & Brown, 1987), it is also the case that such scales do not allow for a fine-grained or temporal analysis of interactive behavior. In addition, this coding approach is not well-suited for the analysis of nonlinear associations between variables; for example, optimal responsiveness or emotion sharing may occur at the midrange of interactive behavior (e.g., Beebe et al., 2008), rather than at the highest or lowest ends.

Finally, it is important to note that mother-toddler dyads were observed at only one time point and causal links between parent-child emotion processes and child behavior problems cannot be inferred; that is, children's poor engagement or involvement in negative emotional exchanges with caregivers may emerge as a *result* of their early internalizing or externalizing difficulties, rather than as a cause thereof. On the other hand, a bi-directional and transactional perspective is core to the study of early childhood mental health; development shapes and is shaped by relationships and it is likely that the dimensions of mother-toddler interaction assessed in this study both affect and are affected by children's behavioral adjustmentThese limitations notwithstanding, findings of the present study suggest several avenues for future research and clinical application. Clinically, findings support the practice of assessing young children within the context of their close relationships and across varying interactive conditions. That is, clinicians or researchers interested

---

[3]   We appreciated the comments of an anonymous reviewer who suggested these more nuanced approaches to the use of self-reported maternal depression data.

in young children at risk for early behavioral problems would be advised to observe children and caregivers in situations that vary in their emotional demands.

Findings also suggest that a full understanding of these early dyadic processes necessarily includes appreciation for the dyadic management of negative
emotions, as well as the capacity to generate and reciprocate positive emotion. As
such, pyscho-educational and clinical efforts aimed at young families should include attention to the full range of emotions as experienced and expressed within
parent-child interactions.

Emotion processes have been increasingly viewed as relational in nature and
as core to the development of childhood psychopathology. A focus on emotions
within dyadic interaction provides a rich approach to conceptualizing the earliest
expressions of internalizing and externalizing problem behaviors and provides a
window through which to view these early problem behaviors. In addition, findings of this study suggest that we may be able to identify specific dyadic processes
that are differentially associated with internalizing and externalizing symptoms,
particularly when consideration is given to the contextual and situational factors
that help to shape the emotional tone and course of parent-toddler interaction.
Intervention services to meet the needs of young children and their families is
in the best interests of those families, their communities, and society as a whole.

References

Achenbach, T., Edelbrock, C., & Howell, C. (1987). Empirically based assessment of the behavioral/emotional problems of 2- and 3-year-old children. *Journal of Abnormal Child Psychology, 15*, 629–650.

Bakeman, R., & Brown, J. (1980). Early interaction: Consequences for social and mental development at three years. *Child Development, 51*, 437–447.

Beebe, B., Jaffe, J., Buck, K., Chen, H., Cohen, P., Blatt, S.,...Andrews, H. (2007). Six-week postpartum maternal self-criticism and dependency and 4-month mother-infant self- and interactive contingencies. *Developmental Psychology, 43*, 1360–1376.

Beebe, B., Jaffe, J., Buck, K., Chen, H., Cohen, P., Feldstein, S., & Andreas, H. (2008). Six-week postpartum maternal depressive symptoms and 4-month mother-infant self- and interactive contingency. *Infant Mental Health Journal, 29*, 442–472.

Belsky, J., Hsieh, K. H., & Crnic, K. A. (1998). Mothering, fathering, and infant negativity as antecedents of boys' externalizing problems and inhibition at 3 years: Differential susceptibility to rearing experience? *Development and Psychopathology, 10*, 301–319.

Belsky, J., Woodward, S., & Crnic, K. A. (1996). Trouble in the second year: Three questions about family interaction. *Child Development, 67*, 556 – 578.

Biringen, Z. (2000). Emotional availability: Conceptualization and research findings. *American Journal of Orthopsychiatry, 70*, 104–114.

Biringen, Z., Damon, J., Grigg, W., Monte, J., Pipp-Siegel, S., Skillern, S., & Stratton, J. (2005). Emotional availability: Differential predictions to infant attachment and kindergarten adjustment based on observation time and context. *Infant Mental Health Journal, 26*, 295–308.

Briggs-Gowan, M. J., Carter, A. S., Bosson-Hennan, J., Guver, A. E., & Horwitz, S. M. (2006). Are infant-toddler social-emotional and behavioral problems transient? *Journal of the American Academy of Child and Adolescent Psychiatry, 45*, 849–858.

Carmichael-Olson, H., Greenberg, M., & Slough, N. (1985). *Coding manual for the Waiting Task.* Unpublished manual, Department of Psychology, University of Washington.

Carter, A. S., Godoy, L., Wagmiller, R. L., Phillip, V., Marakovitz, S., & Briggs-Gowen, M. J. (2010). Internalizing trajectories in boys and girls: The whole is not a simple sum of its parts. *Journal of Abnormal Child Psychology, 38*, 19–31.

Caughy, M. O., Huang, K., & Lima, J. (2009). Patterns of conflict interaction in mother-toddler dyads: Differences between depressed and non-depressed mothers. *Journal of Child and Family Studies, 18*, 10–20.

Cole, P. M., & Deater-Deckard, K. (2009). Emotion regulation, risk, and psycho-pathology. *Journal of Child Psychology and Psychiatry, 50*, 1327–1330.

Cole, P. M., Dennis, T. A., Martin, S. E., & Hall, S. E. (2008). Emotion regulation and the early development of psychopathology. In M. Vandekerckhove, C. von Scheve, S. Ismer, S. Jung, & S. Kronast, (Eds.), *Regulating Emotions: Culture, Social Necessity, and Biological Inheritance.* Malden, MA: Blackwell.

Cole, P. M., Luby, J., & Sullivan, M. W. (2008). Emotions and the development of childhood depression: Bridging the gap. *Child Development Perspectives, 2*, 141–148.

Cole, P. M., Michel, M., & Teti, L. (1994). The development of emotion regula-tion: A clinical perspective. *Monographs of the Society for Research in Child Development, 59* (2–3), 73–100.

Cole, P. M., Teti, L. O., & Zahn-Waxler, C. (2003). Mutual emotion regulation and the stability of conduct problems between preschool and early school age. *Development and Psychopathology, 15*, 1–18.

Criss, M. M., Shaw, D. S., & Ingoldsby, E. M. (2003). Mother-son positive syn-chrony in middle childhood: Relation to antisocial behavior. *Social Deve-lopment, 12*, 379–400.

Deater-Deckard, K., Atzaba-Poria, N., & Pike, A. (2004). Mother- and father-child mutuality in Anglo and Indian British families: A link with lower externalizing problems. *Journal of Abnormal Child Psychology, 32*, 609–620.

Deater-Deckard, K., & Petrill, S. A. (2004). Parent-child dyadic mutuality and child behavior problems: An investigation of gene-environment processes. *Journal of Child Psychology and Psychiatry, 45*, 1171–1179.

Dennis, T. A., Cole, P. M., Wiggins, C. N., Cohen, L. H., & Zalewski, M. (2009). The functional organization of preschool-age children's emotion expressions and actions in challenging situations. *Emotion, 9*, 520–530.

Dix, T., & Meunier, L. N. (2009). Depressive symptoms and parenting competence: An analysis of 13 regulatory processes. *Developmental Review, 29*, 45–68.

Downey, G., & Coyne, J. (1990). Children of depressed parents: An integrative review. *Psychological Bulletin, 108*, 50–76.

Elgar, F. J., McGrath, P. J., Waschbusch, D. A., Steward, S. H., & Curtis, L. J. (2004). Mutual influences on maternal depression and child adjustment problems. *Clinical Psychology Review, 24*, 441–459.

Feng, X., Shaw, D. S., Skuban, E. M., & Lane, T. (2007). Emotional exchange in mother-child dyads: Stability, mutual influence, and associations with mater-nal depression and child problem behavior. *Journal of Family Psychology, 21*, 714-725.

Fogel, A. (1993). *Developing through relationships: Origins of communication, self, and culture.* Chicago: University of Chicago Press.

Frick, P. J., & Morris, A. S. (2004). Temperament and developmental pathways to conduct problems. *Journal of Clinical Child and Adolescent Psychology, 33*, 54–68.

Gartstein, M. A., & Bateman, A. E. (2008). Early manifestations of childhood depression: Influences of infant temperament and depressive symptoms. *Infant and Child Development, 17*, 223–248.

Grolnick, W. S., Bridges, L. J., & Connell, J. P. (1996). Emotion regulation in two-year-olds: Strategies and emotional expression in four contexts. *Child Development, 67*, 928–941.

Harrist, A. W., Petit, G. S., Dodge, K. A., & Bates, J. E. (1994). Dyadic synchrony in mother-child interaction: Relation with children's subsequent kindergarten adjustment. *Family Relations, 43*, 417–424.

Harrist, A. W., & Waugh, R. M. (2002). Dyadic synchrony: Its structure and function in children's development. *Developmental Review, 22*, 555–592.

Izard, C. E., Youngstrom, E. A., Fine, S. E., Mostow, A. J., & Trentacosta, C. J. (2006). Emotions and developmental psychopathology. In D. Cicchetti & D. Cohen (Eds.), *Developmental psychopathology, Vol 1: Theory and method* (2nd ed.) (pp. 244–292). Hoboken, NJ, US: John Wiley & Sons Inc.

Jameson, P. B., Gelfand, D. M., Kulscar, E., & Teti, D. M. (1997). Mother-toddler interaction patterns associated with maternal depression. *Development and Psychopathology, 9*, 537–550.

Keenan, K., & Wakschlag, L. S. (2000). More than the terrible twos: The nature and severity of behavior problems in clinic-referred preschool children. *Journal of Abnormal Child Psychology, 28*, 33–46.

Kochanska, G. (1997). Mutually responsive orientation between mothers and their young children: Implications for early socialization. *Child Development, 68*, 94–112.

Leckman-Westin, E., Cohen, P. R., & Stueve, A. (2009). Maternal depression and mother-child interaction patterns: Association with toddler problems and continuity of effects to late childhood. *Journal of Child Psychology and Psychiatry, 50*, 1176–1184.

Leech, N. L., Barrett, K. C., & Morgan, G. A. (2008). *SPSS for Intermediate Statistics: Use and Interpretation* (3rd ed.). Mahwah, NJ: Lawrence Erlbaum Associates.

Lehman, E. B., Steier, A. J., Guidash, K. M., & Wanna, S. Y. (2002). Predictors of compliance in toddlers: Child temperament, maternal personality, and emotional availability. *Early Child Development and Care, 172*, 301–310.

Lindsey, E. W., Cremeens, P. R., & Caldera, Y. M. (2010). Mother-child and father-child mutuality in two contexts: Consequences for young children's peer relationships. *Infant and Child Development, 19*, 142–160.

Lindsey, E. W., Cremeens, P. R., Colwell, M. J., & Caldera, Y. M. (2009). The structure of parent-child dyadic synchrony in toddlerhood and children's communication competence and self-control. *Social Development, 18*, 375–396.

Lindsey, E. W., Mize, J., & Petit, G. S. (1997). Mutuality in parent-child play: Consequences for children's peer competence. *Journal of Social and Personal Relationships, 14*, 523–538.

Luby, J. (2009). Depression. In C. H. Zeanah (Ed.), *Handbook of Infant Mental Health* (3rd ed.) (pp. 409–420). New York: Guildford Press.

Lyons-Ruth, K., Wolfe, R., Lyubchik, A., & Steingard, R. (2002). Depressive symptoms in parents of children under age 3: Sociodemographic predictors, current correlates, and associated parenting behaviors. In N. Halfon, K. T. McLearn, & M. A. Schuster (Eds.), *Child Rearing in America: Challenges Facing Parents with Young Children* (pp. 217–259). New York: Cambridge University Press.

Martin, S. E., Clements, M. L., & Crnic, K. A. (2002). Maternal emotions during mother-toddler interaction: Parenting in affective context. *Parenting: Science and Practice, 2*, 105-126.

NICHD Early Child Care Research Network (2004). Affect dysregulation in the mother–child relationship in the toddler years: Antecedents and consequences. *Development and Psychopathology, 16*, 43–68.

Pickens, J., & Field, T. (1993). Facial expressivity in infants of "depressed" mothers. *Developmental Psychology, 29*, 986–988.

Radloff, L. (1977). The CES-D Scale: A self-report depression scale for research in the general population. *Applied Psychological Measurement, 1*, 385 – 401.

Raver, C. C. (1996). Relations between social contingency in mother-child interaction and 2-year-olds' social competence. *Developmental Psychology, 32*, 850–859.

Reck, C., Hunt, A., Fuchs, T., Weiss, R., Noon, A., Moehler, E.,...Mundt, C. (2004). Interactive regulation of affect in postpartum depressed mothers and their infants: An overview. *Psychopathology, 37*, 272–280.

Rocissano, L., Slade, A., & Lynch, V. (1987). Dyadic synchrony and toddler compliance. *Developmental Psychology, 23*, 698–704.

Rodriguez, M. L., Ayduk, O., Aber, J. L., Mischel, W., Sethi, A., & Shoda, Y. (2005). A contextual approach to the development of self-regulatory competencies: The role of maternal unresponsivity and toddlers' negative affect in stressful situations. *Social Development, 14*, 136–157.

Santor, D., Zuroff, D., Ramsay, J., Cervantes, P., & Palacios, J. (1995). Examining the scale discriminability in the BDI and CES-D as a function of depressive severity. *Psychological Assessment, 2*, 122–128.

Scaramella, L. V., & Leve, L. D. (2004). Clarifying parent-child reciprocities during early childhood: The early childhood coercion model. *Clinical Child and Family Psychology Review, 7*, 89–107.

Shaw, D. S., Keenan, K., Vondra, J. I., Delliquadri, E., & Giovannelli, J. (1997). Antecedents of preschool children's internalizing problems: A longitudinal study of low-income families. *Journal of the American Academy of Child and Adolescent Psychiatry, 36*, 1760–1767.

Silk, J. S., Shaw, D. S., Forbes, E. E., Lane, T. L., & Kovacs, M. (2006). Maternal depression and child internalizing: The moderating role of child emotion regulation. *Journal of Clinical Child and Adolescent Psychology, 35*, 116–126.

Skuban, E. M., Shaw, D. S., Gardner, F., Supplee, L. H., & Nichols, S. R. (2006). The correlates of dyadic synchrony in high-risk, low-income toddler boys. *Infant Behavior and Development, 29*, 423–434.

Smith, C. L., Calkins, S. D., & Keane, S. P. (2006). The relation of maternal behavior and attachment security to toddlers' emotions and emotion regulation. *Research in Human Development, 3*, 21–31.

Sroufe, A. (1996). *Emotional development: The organization of emotional life in the early years.* Cambridge: University Press.

Stansbury, K., & Sigman, M. (2000). Responses of preschoolers in two frustrating episodes: Emergence of complex strategies for emotion regulation. *Journal of Genetic Psychology, 161*, 182–202.

Tronick, E. (1989). Emotions and emotional communication in infancy. *American Psychologist, 44*, 112–119.

Tronick, E. Z., Beeghly, M., Weinberg, M. K., & Olson, K. L (1997). Postpartum exuberance: Not all women in a highly positive emotional state in the postpartum period are denying depression and distress. *Infant Mental Health Journal, 18*, 406-423.

Wakschlag, L. S., & Danis, B. (2009). Characterizing early childhood disruptive behavior: Enhancing developmental sensitivity. In C. H. Zeanah (Ed.), *Handbook of Infant Mental Health* (3rd ed.) (pp. 392–408). New York: Guilford Press.

West, A. E., & Newman, D. L. (2003). Worried and blue: Mild parental anxiety and depression in relation to the development of young children's temperament and behavior problems. *Parenting: Science and Practice, 3*, 133–154.

Wood, A. M., Taylor, P. J., & Joseph, S. (2010). Does the CES-D measure a continuum from depression to happiness? Comparing substantive and artifactual models. *Psychiatry Research, 177*, 120–123.

Zeman, J., Shipman, K., & Suveg, C. (2002). Anger and sadness regulation: Predictions to internalizing and externalizing symptoms in children. *Journal of Clinical Child and Adolescent Psychology, 31*, 393–398.

Zeanah, C. H. (2009). *Handbook of infant mental health* (3rd ed.). New York: Guilford Press.

Zimmerman, L. K., & Stansbury, K. (2003). The influence of temperamental reactivity and situational context on the emotion-regulatory abilities of 3-year-old children. *Journal of Genetic Psychology, 164*, 389–409.

www.ingramcontent.com/pod-product-compliance
Lightning Source LLC
Chambersburg PA
CBHW071134280326
41935CB00010B/1219